A Young Man's Guide to Self-Mastery

A Young Man's Guide to Self-Mastery

PARTICIPANT'S WORKBOOK

Stephanie S. Covington, PhD, LCSW

Roberto A. Rodriguez, MA, LMFT, LADC

JB JOSSEY-BASS™

A Wiley Brand

Registered Office(s)

John Wiley & Sons, Inc., 111 River Street, Hoboken, NJ 07030, USA

Editorial Office

111 River Street, Hoboken, NJ 07030, USA

For details of our global editorial offices, customer services, and more information about Wiley products visit us at www.wiley.com.

Wiley also publishes its books in a variety of electronic formats and by print-on-demand. Some content that appears in standard print versions of this book may not be available in other formats.

Library of Congress Cataloging-in-Publication Data is Available:

ISBN 9781119627753 (Paperback)
ISBN 9781119627760 (ePDF)
ISBN 9781119627777 (epub)

Cover Design: Wiley
Cover Image: © Banana Oil/Shutterstock

Set in 10.5/15 pt Metropolis by SPi Global, Chennai, India

SKY10037619_102822

This is a gender-expansive program
designed for a wide range of youth,
including those who are transgender
or nonbinary. It is also for those who
are gay or bisexual. It is for all
of you who are experiencing the
world from a masculine perspective.

TABLE OF CONTENTS

Module D: Healthy Living

Module E: Appendices

INTRODUCTION TO YOUR WORKBOOK

A Young Man's Guide to Self-Mastery Participant's Workbook contains information, activities related to your group's sessions, and places for you to make notes about your experiences and reactions. You will use this workbook during your group's sessions and for activities to be done between the sessions.

Don't worry about your handwriting or spelling or drawing ability. This workbook is yours alone. It is a tool for you, and no one will grade it or criticize it. No one else has to see it, and you can decide how much of your work you want to share with the group. As you learn to trust the other group members, you may decide to share more of your work and wisdom in order to compare life experiences, realizations, and decisions you make.

Your group will meet for fourteen sessions. Each session will run for two hours, without a break.

You will use this workbook in several ways:

1. During the sessions, the facilitator may ask you to look at a page in the workbook and to read along with an important piece of information or list.

2. As part of an activity in a session, you may be asked to write or draw in your workbook.

3. At the end of each session in the workbook, there is a place for you to note what you want to remember about that session. This is called "Reflections."

4. After Session One, and through Session Thirteen, you will be asked to complete a "Between-Sessions Activity." This usually means practicing something you learned during the session or writing or drawing about something that happened during the session.

Your honest responses will enable you to look back at where you were and ahead to where you are going. They will provide you with a reminder of what you have learned. You will begin to see your unique strengths and, we hope, a vision of a better future.

Myself

Welcome, Introductions, and Building Our House

THIS SESSION

Your facilitator's name is _____ .

Your co-facilitator is _____ .

Your group will meet _____ .

This program was created to help you use your inner strengths, to master difficulties in your life, and to improve the way you get along with others. The program will help you find a new way to look at issues you have faced in the past and issues you are facing in the present. You will help to create a space in which all of your group members can learn from one another and from the activities and information provided by the facilitator.

In your group, you'll hear things that you have in common with the other participants and things that are different. You have a chance to connect with other people who have been living lives of unique challenges and accomplishments. Most important, you will have a chance to share your thoughts, feelings, and experiences. You won't have to share anything you don't feel comfortable sharing. You'll find a place to be heard and to be supported by others who can relate to you.

This is also a space for you to present yourself as you really are and to explore who you hope to become. Young people come in all shapes, styles, backgrounds, and presentations. This is a place to be your genuine self while supporting others who are doing the same thing. Although we sometimes use the terms "boys and young men" in our discussions to explain how they typically are raised and, therefore, how they may act, this program is created for boys, young men, young trans men and boys, and nonbinary and gender nonconforming people who have a masculine experience of the world.

BEING IN A GROUP

Starting in a new group is not comfortable. You may feel nervous or uneasy and you may try different ways of dealing with your feelings. These are called "defensive strategies." Your facilitators have worked with many people like you and understand your discomfort. They will try to make this an environment in which you feel comfortable and safe and can let others see the real you.

Many of your group members may have experienced trauma or other troubling things in their lives. In this program, you will explore how violence, abuse, trauma, power, control, and powerlessness are part of the lives of many young people. It will help you to identify your inner strengths and talents in order to master the difficulties that you may be facing. Then you can discover how to lead a healthier life and have healthier relationships with yourself and others. Most important, you will begin to have a sense of mastery of yourself and your future.

MUTUAL AGREEMENTS

Some of the qualities that groups like yours name as being important are trust, confidentiality, respect, collaboration, nonjudgment, compassion, empathy, and acceptance. These, and whatever your group chooses to add, will be the foundations of your work together.

You can list your group's building blocks here:

THE WORD CLOUD

A Word Cloud is a way of tracking words that are used most often by people on social networks. The more a word is used, the larger it is.

On the next page, use words that describe you and your interests to make a Word Cloud. The more a word is true of you, the bigger it should be. Words that say more about you are horizontal on the page, and words that aren't so obvious may be vertical, upside down, or backwards. You choose the direction that fits you. You can use colors for emphasis. You also may draw symbols or pictures instead of using words. Here is a sample.

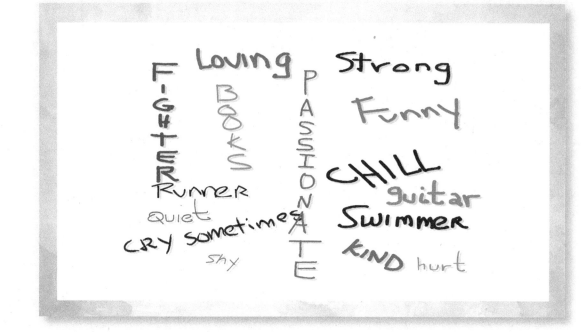

FIVE SENSES

A "grounding" activity can help you to detach from your inner, emotional discomfort by helping you to be more aware of the physical world and connecting with the "here and now." It is one of the self-mastery techniques you will learn in this program.

1. Close your eyes or lower your eyelids.
2. Relax for a few moments. Take a few deep breaths and exhale slowly.
3. Open your eyes when you're ready.
4. Silently, identify five things you can see around you.
5. Now identify four things you can feel or touch.
6. Identify three things you can hear.
7. Now identify two things you can smell.
8. Finally, identify what you can taste right now.
9. Now focus your eyes on something in front of you and mentally come back into the present.

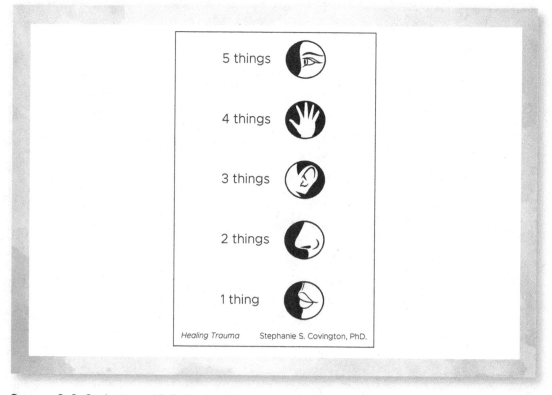

5 things

4 things

3 things

2 things

1 thing

Healing Trauma   Stephanie S. Covington, PhD.

Source: S. S. Covington with E. Russo. (2016). *Healing Trauma: A Brief Intervention for Women* (Rev. ed.). (p. 161). Center City, MN: Hazelden.

REFLECTION

"Reflection" is thinking deeply or carefully about something. Think back to what had the most impact on you in today's session, what you felt, and what you want to remember. Here is a space for you to write or draw about it. You may finish this after the session ends.

BETWEEN-SESSIONS ACTIVITY

Take time between now and the next session to practice the Five Senses grounding technique at least once per day. Be ready to share about your experience with this activity in the next session. You may want to make some notes about it on this page. You may also want to complete your Reflection activity.

A Sense of Self

THIS SESSION

All of the people in your group have had experiences that influence how they think of themselves and how they interact with the world. This session is intended to help you become more aware of the many things that have contributed to your sense of "self" and the ways in which you relate to others.

MY PLACE

You can practice this grounding technique in many situations, especially when you want to calm down. Many people say that this works well in situations when they're feeling stressed, frustrated, or angry.

1. Sit comfortably but with good posture, with your back straight, and place your feet flat on the floor.

2. Place your hands either palms up or palms down on your lap and relax. You may close your eyes if you're comfortable with that or you may choose to focus on a fixed spot on the floor directly in front of you.

3. Relax your shoulders and slowly roll your neck in a circle from left to right.

4. Now roll your neck in a circle from right to left.

5. Holding your head still, allow yourself to notice how you're breathing.

6. Then inhale gently through your nose and exhale fully through your mouth.

7. Feel the temperature of the air as it comes in through your nose.

8. Feel the air as it leaves your body when you breathe out through your mouth.

9. Don't force your breath; let it flow naturally and slowly.

10. If you begin to think about different things that are happening in your life outside this room, just notice them without judgment and let them drift past like clouds in the sky as you return to noticing your breath.

11. Continue to be aware of your breath as it slowly flows in and out.

12. Now, choose an image of a place that means calmness or safety to you. It can be a real place or you can use your imagination.

13. Take a moment to breathe in all the beauty of this place.

14. Then breathe out any negative or distracting thoughts you may have had when you came here today.

15. Repeat breathing in your calm or safe place and breathing out any negative thoughts.

16. Do this a few more times.

17. When you're ready, return to the here and now and focus on the present.

MY PLACE (VARIATION)

1. Sit quietly and let yourself relax.

2. You may close your eyes or look at a fixed spot on the floor directly in front of you.

3. Put one hand on your chest and one hand on your stomach.

4. Take a couple of normal breaths. You probably will find that you are feeling these breaths mostly in your chest.

5. Try moving your breath deeper into your lower abdomen so that your hand on your stomach moves as you breathe.

6. Close your mouth and press your tongue lightly to the roof of your mouth. Let your jaw relax.

7. Take a breath slowly in through your nose as you silently count to four.

8. Slowly exhale and feel the breath leaving your nose as you silently count to four one more time.

9. Try it again.

10. As thoughts come up, acknowledge them and then return your focus to your breathing.

11. Keep breathing deeply. Let your belly fill with air each time.

12. Breathe in through your nose and count to four.

13. Breath out slowly, counting to four.

14. Now, picture a place in your mind that means peace or calm to you. It can be a place you've been to before or one you imagine.

15. Only you are there, no one else.

16. As you continue to breathe, take in the beauty of this place,
    - the temperature,
    - the sounds,
    - and the way you feel when you are here.

17. This is your place, where you can be safe, where nothing can harm you.

18. You can come here anytime simply by closing your eyes and breathing as you've practiced.

19. Now, slowly become more aware of the room and, when you are ready, open your eyes.

FEELINGS, BELIEFS, AND VALUES

1. Who were the people that influenced the way you see yourself today?

_____

_____

_____

_____

_____

_____

_____

_____

2. What are the places you've been that you really remember and why do you remember them?

_____

_____

_____

_____

_____

_____

_____

_____

3. What experiences do you think have shaped your feelings, beliefs, and values?

_____

_____

_____

_____

_____

_____

_____

_____

4. What are some of your values?

_____

_____

_____

_____

_____

_____

_____

_____

MY CASTLE (OUTSIDE)

Use the insights you gained from the last activity to draw a castle that shows how you interact with your world. If you are a trusting person, your castle may not have tall or thick walls, may not have a moat to protect it, and may not have guard towers. If you are more cautious or don't trust so easily, your walls may be higher and there may be archers in the tower and a moat or drawbridge to protect your castle. You can use words as well as drawings.

MY CASTLE (INSIDE)

Also imagine what the inside of your castle looks like. Is it different than the outside? You decide: Are there windows, gates, doors, decorations? What parts of you or feelings are you protecting? Who is in the castle with you?

REFLECTION

Here is a space for you to write or draw about what meant the most to you in your group today. What do you want to remember? You may finish this after the session ends.

BETWEEN-SESSIONS ACTIVITY

Take time between now and the next session to answer the following questions:

1. What are the personal values you listed in your group discussion?

_____

_____

_____

_____

_____

_____

_____

_____

2. What are some ways in which your behaviors match and also don't match your values?

_____

_____

_____

_____

_____

_____

_____

_____

3. What are some changes you can make so that what you do matches what you value?

_____

_____

_____

_____

_____

_____

_____

_____

_____

_____

_____

_____

_____

_____

_____

_____

_____

Be ready to share about your experience with this in the next session.

A Boy's World

THIS SESSION

We often learn what it means to be a man from our fathers, our mothers, men in our neighborhoods, and other adults in our lives. We also are influenced by television, movies, social media, and peers (people our age). People raised as boys often are taught to play violent and aggressive games. They experience peer violence more often than girls do. People who grow up in households where there is substance misuse, financial stress, and/or mental illness may experience abuse, neglect, and violence. They may learn that the only way to achieve safety and security is through showing power by verbal and physical aggression.

This session helps you to examine the messages you have received about masculinity. You will explore difficulties associated with ideas about sexual orientation and gender.

This session also can help you to identify and express some of your emotions.

Here is some extra space for you to doodle, sketch or write...

PALMS UP, PALMS DOWN

Here is another technique to help you concentrate and stay present in the moment.

1. Sit up straight in your seat, with both feet on the floor and your eyes closed. If you're not comfortable closing your eyes, look at a spot in front of you on the floor.
2. Breathe naturally and slowly.
3. Now begin to breathe deeper into your belly.
4. Breathe in to a count of four.
5. Breathe out to a count of six.
6. Repeat that a couple of times.
7. Now, hold both your arms outstretched, with the palms of your hands turned up and touching side by side, as though someone was about to put something in your hands.
8. Visualize a list of all the thoughts and feelings that are bothering you right now.
9. Now imagine placing all your cares, concerns, problems, and troubling memories into your hands.
10. All these negative emotions and thoughts are out of your bodies and lying in your hands.
11. Imagine the weight of holding all these problems, these negative thoughts and emotions, in your hands. Feel the strain of carrying them.
12. Now, slowly and carefully turn your hands upside down, so that your palms face the floor. Let all the problems, stresses, bad feelings, and negativity fall to the floor. For now, drop everything that might distract you from what you need to do.
13. When you are ready, open your eyes.

COLLAGE OF GENDER EXPECTATIONS

A collage is a piece of art made with different materials, such as cut-out pictures, words, and drawings. Divide your poster board into two parts, one side for girls and one side for boys. Use the magazines and cut out or tear out pictures and words that show society's expectations of girls and boys. It doesn't matter how you were raised. You probably experienced this type of pressure, even if you knew the expectations were wrong for you. If you are an individual who is not connected with being a boy or girl, you will want to think about your experiences in a world that focuses on boys and girls when this may not fit for you. You can glue pictures and words to your poster board and fill in with your crayons or colored pencils. If you are artistic, you can just draw on your board.

Use these three questions to guide you as you create your collage:

1. How are boys and girls treated differently as children?

2. Social messages come from many sources, including family members, teachers, movies, music, and video games. What are the social messages that boys get? How are boys supposed to act?

_____

_____

_____

_____

_____

_____

_____

_____

3. What are the social media messages that girls get? How are girls supposed to act?

_____

_____

_____

_____

_____

_____

_____

_____

THE ANGER FUNNEL

1. Someone says or does something that upsets or distresses us.
2. We think about what happened.
3. We feel an emotion. It may actually be fear or sadness or disappointment, but we typically don't know how to separate or handle those emotions, so we identify it as anger.

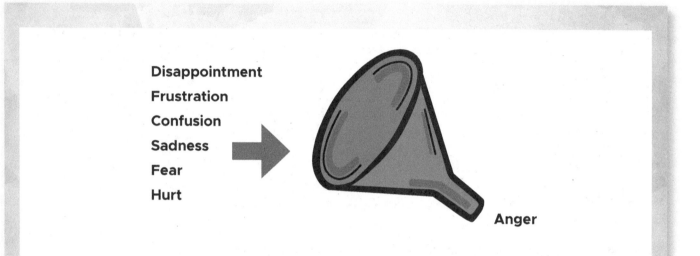

Disappointment
Frustration
Confusion
Sadness
Fear
Hurt

Anger

Anger can be felt on a continuum from annoyance to anger to rage, which can lead to violence.

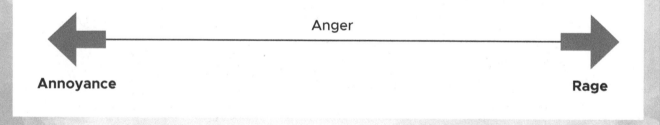

Anger

Annoyance

Rage

THE CONTAINER

Here is a useful technique for when you are feeling overwhelmed but can't do anything about it at the time. It helps you to "contain" what you are feeling until you can find a better time to express it.

1. Sit comfortably with good posture, with your feet on the ground and your hands in a comfortable position on your lap.
2. You may close your eyes if you are comfortable doing so or lower your gaze to focus on a spot directly in front of you.
3. Tune in to your breathing. Slowly and smoothly breathe in.
4. Feel the temperature of the air as it passes into your lungs.
5. Exhale slowly and smoothly.
6. Continue breathing in and out smoothly.
7. Now imagine a container. It can be any object, any shape you want. It only has to have a lid to hold things securely inside.
8. As you continue to breathe deeply and smoothly, become aware of any powerful emotions you may feel right now. These may include feelings of hurt or shame or frustration or whatever.
9. Slowly, one by one, place all these feelings inside your container.
10. Once you've placed all of them in the container, tightly close the lid.
11. These feelings or emotions have not gone away. You're just putting them inside the container for now so that you can interact with the world around you in the present. You can deal with these feelings and emotions later when it is a better time to do so.
12. When you've closed your container and are ready, return to the here and now. You can draw a picture of your container on the next page.

REFLECTION

Reflect on what was meaningful to you in this session and what you want to remember. Then write or draw about it here.

BETWEEN-SESSIONS ACTIVITY

Sometime between now and the next session, if you become angry, take time to practice with your own Anger Funnel on the next page.

1. Write or draw what happened or what was said [the event] in the section below.
2. Write what you thought and felt about it on the next page.
3. Try to identify and list the emotions you felt before the anger and put those on the left, at the top of the funnel.
4. Next, place a mark on the line to indicate how much anger you felt.
5. Then, on the right side of the funnel, list any thoughts you might have thought instead so that you would not be as angry.

What happened?

What did you think?

_____

_____

_____

_____

_____

_____

_____

_____

_____

_____

What did you feel?

_____

_____

_____

_____

_____

_____

_____

_____

_____

_____

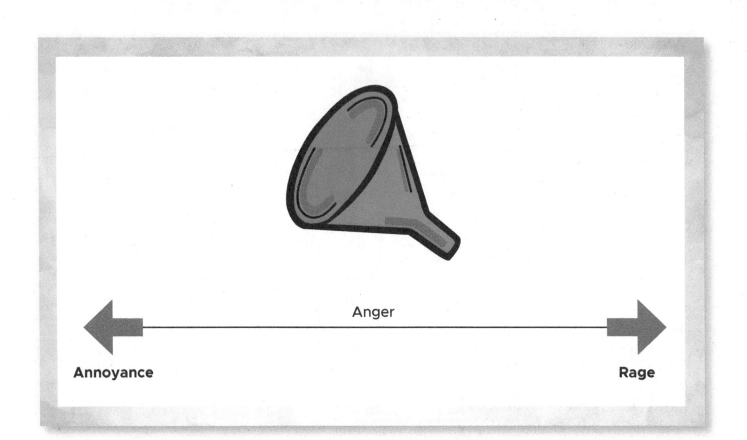

Anger

Annoyance ←——————————————————————————→ Rage

Introduction to Trauma

THIS SESSION

Many young people have never learned how to manage their responses to problems. This may have led to trouble and caused some of them to blame themselves for responses they had no control over.

Many young people also face problems ranging from challenging home environments, lack of economic resources, lack of proper nutrition, and lack of educational opportunities to overwhelming and horrifying experiences, including physical and verbal violence in their homes and neighborhoods.

In this session, you can explore the effects of traumatic experiences, examine your present adaptive strategies, and begin to think about developing more effective ones.

THE FIGHT-OR-FLIGHT RESPONSE

When we see or hear something that threatens us, our ears and eyes send a signal to the brain. The brain sends a signal to the adrenal glands. The adrenal glands pump a bunch of adrenalin into the blood system. When it reaches the heart, it begins to pump a lot of blood to the big muscles in the arms and legs, helping us to either run from the danger or attack it. This means that the front part of the brain that does our thinking temporarily shuts down, because the survival part of the brain takes over.

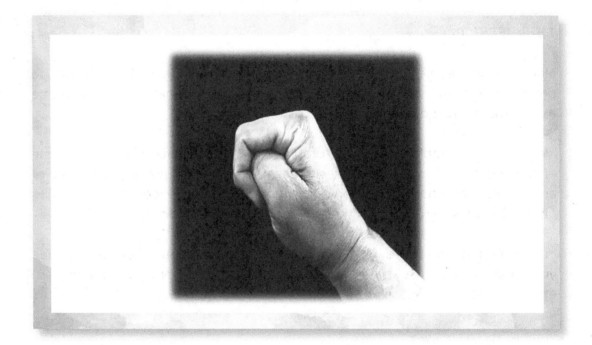

Looking at this hand from the side, you can see that it resembles a brain. The fingers represent the part of the brain that is responsible for all the serious and critical thinking. It warns you and helps you to solve difficult problems. The thumb area represents the limbic system. This is where a lot of the emotions live.

A part of the brain that signals the adrenal glands also is here. You may have noticed that when you are feeling threatened, or are about to fight, you feel "butterflies" in your stomach. You may know of athletes who throw up before a game. This is because a lot of adrenaline is being pumped into the blood system.

Look at the hand again. The wrist looks like the brain stem. It's the part of the brain called the "reptilian" or "old" brain. This part is mostly responsible for all the physical things your body does without you having to think about them, such as blinking, breathing, flinching, and so on.

Think of the last time you felt really angry or threatened. Chances are that the limbic and the reptilian parts of your brain reacted automatically. That means that the pre-frontal cortex (the thinking part of your brain) quit working properly.

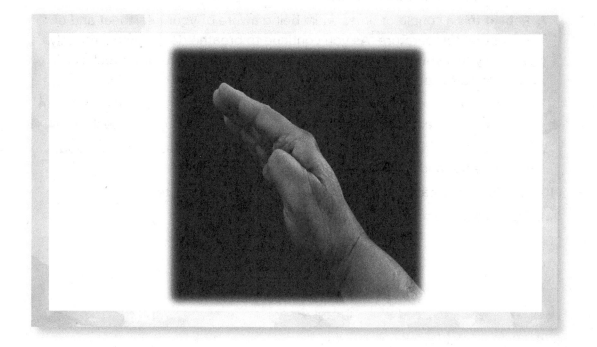

This is where the saying "flip your lid" came from. When you are very angry or feel threatened, your limbic and reptilian brains take over, and all you can think about is how to win or survive, by either running or fighting. You can see why it's so hard to think clearly when you are angry.

BREATHING

If you can take deep, slow breaths when you are angry or threatened, you can slow everything else down. The adrenaline will stop pumping, your heart will slow down, your temperature will cool down, and your muscles will relax. If you can master your breathing, you can begin to use your higher brain to master your reaction to what is troubling you.

1. Sit comfortably, with your back straight and your feet flat on the ground.
2. If you're comfortable doing so, shut your eyes. Otherwise, focus your eyes on a spot on the ground.

3. Next, become aware of your body. Scan your body for any sensations or tension you may feel.

4. Then go inside your body and focus on your heartbeat and your body temperature.

5. Begin breathing deeply but smoothly. It may help if you count to four when you breathe in.

6. Next, exhale to the count of six.

7. Repeat this a couple of times while being aware of your heartbeat and of your body temperature. As you continue to breathe deeply and smoothly, you may feel your heartbeat slow down and your temperature feel warm and comfortable.

8. As you continue to breathe deeply and slowly, you may feel that the sensation or tension you felt before may be beginning to ease and that you feel calmer.

9. Continue to breathe while relaxing all your facial muscles: your forehead, your cheeks, and your jaw.

10. Continue to breathe and enjoy this moment of self-mastery.

11. Open your eyes and return to the here and now.

TRAUMA

Trauma affects all sorts of people, and each may respond to trauma differently. What may be a very traumatic thing for one person may not be felt the same way by another.

For some, the trauma builds over time. For example, some stress can help us get stronger and grow. But if the stress lasts too long, it wears down our bodies, can harm our health, and puts us at risk for engaging in behaviors that aren't good for us or others, such as using alcohol or other drugs, aggressive behavior, and isolating ourselves.

Here are some statistics that show how much trauma can be in a person's life.

- More than one in every nine children are exposed to violence annually in the United States, and one in four children is exposed to family violence.
- In one study, male adults were more likely than female adults to report emotional abuse during childhood and physical abuse during childhood. But females reported sexual abuse at twice the rate of males. Males and females reported about the same amount of physical and emotional neglect.
- Children exposed to family violence commonly experience other adverse childhood experiences, including emotional, physical, and sexual abuse and neglect.
- Men who are abused as children are 50% more likely to continue the cycle of violence as adults. Approximately 50% of boys who witness family violence will perpetrate such abuse and violence as adults.
- Many studies indicate that ongoing exposure to violence on television, on the internet, and in video games during childhood increases aggressive and antisocial behavior, particularly in boys.
- Men who view women being objectified in media images are more likely to engage in sexual coercion and sexual harassment of women.
- Gay men and lesbians have consistently been the third most frequent targets of hate violence.
- Of the estimated 800,000 gang members in the United States, 90% are male. Gang-related offenses committed with firearms account for at least 95% of crime in gang-controlled areas.
- Lesbian, gay, bisexual, transgender, and gender nonconforming teenagers experience higher rates of bullying, physical and sexual violence, and drug use than do their cisgender heterosexual peers.

Young men who struggle with substance use are more likely to have been victims of childhood physical and sexual abuse than are young men who are not struggling with substance use disorders. Also, young men who struggle with alcohol and other drugs are more likely to abuse others.

Trauma affects our *inner selves*: our thoughts, feelings, beliefs, and values. For example, some of us have been victimized or hurt physically, sexually, mentally, or emotionally. Because of these experiences, we can begin to believe that the world is a dangerous place where we can survive only by feeling powerful and always in control.

Trauma also affects our *outer lives*: our relationships and behaviors. As a result, when we grow older, we can struggle in our relationships with family members, friends, and sexual partners, and we may feel like we don't fit in. We may struggle with maintaining appropriate boundaries, and we may act out sexually.

Many things influence how a young person reacts to a traumatic event: the person's age, history of other trauma, family interactions, support systems, and so on. Someone may be so used to negative things that are happening, like sirens or gunfire in the night, that he may not even recognize them as stressful.

Some young men may see themselves as failures because they weren't able to defend themselves or others from violence or abuse. Others may feel as if they were "ruined" by being sexually abused. Some young men may feel deep shame because of some of the things they've done in attempting to deal with their pain. They may now realize that things they did to feel more powerful and in control were wrong and deeply hurt others.

Posttraumatic Stress Disorder

Some typical symptoms of PTSD are as follows:

- Memories of the bad stuff that happened
- Avoiding reminders of the bad thing that happened
- Feeling irritable or edgy when thinking about the past
- Getting angry easily
- Being very watchful
- Feeling paranoid
- Startling easily
- Jumping when someone comes up behind you
- Flinching when someone touches you
- Having trouble trusting people
- Never really feeling safe
- Feeling numb
- Checking out

"Big T" traumas are those we associate with PTSD and may include the death of someone you know or love, being physically abused, being assaulted, being sexually abused, and surviving a disaster.

"Little t" traumas are those that may not seem as serious at first but may leave a person feeling shameful or as though he is a failure. Examples are being humiliated or bullied, being teased and harassed for being trans, nonbinary or LGBTQI, and being shamed for showing fear, emotions, or sensitivity.

Whether something is a "Big T" or "little t" trauma depends on the perspective of the person who experiences it. You can create a list here of some of the "Big T" and "little t" traumas that are mentioned in your group.

THE ACE QUESTIONNAIRE

The questions on this page and the next one are taken from a survey tool called the ACE Questionnaire. ACE stands for "adverse childhood experiences." Even if you don't think you've had any adverse childhood experiences, fill out the questionnaire anyway. It may help you understand which events in childhood can be traumatic.

When you're finished, please allow others to complete their questions in silence.

If you feel uncomfortable or triggered by these questions, remember to do the breathing technique you practiced earlier or use your Five Senses card.

ACE QUESTIONNAIRE

While you were growing up, during your first 18 years of life:		Yes	No
1.	Did a parent or other adult in the household often swear at you, insult you, put you down, humiliate you, or act in a way that made you afraid that you might be physically hurt? **If yes, enter "1"** ➤____		
2.	Did a parent or other adult in the household often push, grab, or slap you; throw something at you; or ever hit you so hard that you had marks or were injured? **If yes, enter "1"** ➤____		
3.	Did an adult or person at least five years older than you ever touch or fondle you or have you touch his/her body in a sexual way or try to or actually have oral or anal sex with you? **If yes, enter "1"** ➤____		
4.	Did you often feel that no one in your family loved you or thought you were important or special, or that your family members didn't look out for one another, feel close to one another, or support one another? **If yes, enter "1"** ➤____		

(continued)

(continued)

While you were growing up, during your first 18 years of life:	Yes	No
5. Did you often feel that you didn't have enough to eat, had to wear dirty clothes, and had no one to protect you, or that your parents were too drunk or high to take care of you or take you to the doctor? **If yes, enter "1"** ➤___		
6. Have you lost a parent through separation, divorce, or death? **If yes, enter "1"** ➤___		
7. Was your mother or stepmother often pushed, grabbed, or slapped, or did she have something thrown at her? Or was she sometimes or often kicked, bitten, hit with a fist, or hit with something hard? Or was she ever repeatedly hit over at least a few minutes or threatened with a gun or knife? **If yes, enter "1"** ➤___		
8. Did you live with anyone who was a problem drinker or alcoholic or who used street drugs? If yes, enter "1" ➤___		
9. Was a household member depressed or mentally ill or did a household member attempt suicide? **If yes, enter "1"** ➤___		
10. Did a household member go to prison? **If yes, enter "1"** ➤___		
11. Enter the total number of Yes answers here. **This is your ACE score** ➤___		

Source: Adapted from V. J. Felitti. (2000). *One-page ACE Questionnaire Handout.* Self-published. Personal communication with S. Covington on December 7, 2015.

Going through adverse events in childhood puts us at greater risk of having physical and mental health challenges later in life. For instance, people who answer "yes" to four or more of the items are at greatest risk for having ongoing health problems.

A person with a score of four or more "yes" answers is at greater risk for developing a problem with drugs or alcohol as a way of coping with trauma and reducing the stress of living in a violent environment.

OTHER TRAUMATIC EVENTS

There are other types of traumatic events:

- Being abandoned or neglected as a child
- Accidents (cars, bicycles, playgrounds)
- Serious injuries (sports, gunshots, broken bones)
- Inner city, warlike conditions
- Mugging, robbery
- Rape or assault
- Living in fear of being exposed to violence or loss
- Fear of being outed because of your gender or sexual identity
- Being dead named (called the name given before transitioning)
- Gang activity
- Fights, being arrested, being jailed
- Witnessing murders or being forced to commit murder
- Domestic violence or emotional, sexual, or physical abuse
- Death of a loved one (even a pet)
- Immigration
- Historical trauma (intergenerational or cultural) that happens to groups of people; in the US, this includes African Americans, Native Americans, Native Alaskans, and Native Hawaiians

TRAUMA CAN SHAPE OUR BELIEF SYSTEMS

Our belief systems are continually challenged or reinforced by things we see, hear, do, and think about. If we live in a state of toxic stress, our beliefs about the world are going to be very different from those of a person who has not gone through what we have.

If young people_____,

they may grow up to believe _____

_____

_____

_____

_____.

If young people _____,

they may grow up to believe _____

_____

_____

_____

_____

_____

_____

_____ .

If young people _____,

they may grow up to believe _____

_____

_____

_____

_____

_____

_____

_____

_____ .

REFLECTION

Reflect on what was meaningful to you in this session and what you want to remember. Then write or draw about it here.

BETWEEN-SESSIONS ACTIVITY

Sometime between now and the next session, when you find that you are feeling tense or anxious, do the breathing activity that your group did in this session. Remember to scan your body for tension or sensations, then feel your heartbeat and your temperature. As you breathe deeply and smoothly, notice how your heart may slow down and your temperature may cool, and your body sensations may ease.

Communication and Connections

Communication and Connections

THIS SESSION

Young people create ways to deal with their life experiences and situations. Sometimes the things they do to survive do not help them to make meaningful connections with others or to live in tune with their values.

In this session, you have a chance to look at different values and decide which ones you want to live by and what you want to change. You learn about healthy connections with others and barriers to healthy connections. You practice communication skills, such as "reading" other people's facial and body cues and their tones of voice. You learn words that help to express emotions. You gain a deeper awareness of subtle, nonverbal ways in which we express emotions. You also learn the three basic communication styles and practice using assertive communication rather than less effective communication styles.

You also practice new grounding and self-mastery skills that you can use whenever you are feeling stressed or challenged.

HEALING LIGHT

1. Sit up straight in your seat, with both feet on the floor and your eyes closed.
2. Close your eyes if you are comfortable doing so. Otherwise, look at a spot on the floor in front of you.
3. Breathe naturally and slowly.

4. Now begin to breathe deeper into your belly.

5. Breathe in to the count of four.

6. Breathe out to the count of six.

7. Repeat that a couple of times.

8. Now, as you continue to breath, scan your body for any place where you might feel tightness or soreness.

9. Focus on that spot and give the sensation a color. It could be black or dark red or any other color you want.

10. Continue to breathe and now imagine that you can feel a light above you. Give it a color.

11. Allow this healing light to come in through the top of your head and into your shoulders. Let this light travel to where you felt the tightness or soreness before.

12. Continue to breathe deeply and imagine the color of the healing light mixing with the color or your tightness or soreness and then begin to dissolve it.

13. Feel the tension and soreness continue to ease as you breathe for a few more breaths.

14. When you are ready, open your eyes.

- -

LIVING YOUR VALUES

Most of us learn some good values and maybe some not-so-good values when we are growing up. Values are what help us stay connected to one another and to live in families, communities, and civilizations. Now you have a choice. You can decide which values you want to live by and pass on to your children and which you want to change.

On the next page is a place to write the values that your group came up with. You may want to put a star next to the ones that you think are best.

If you continue to do the things you have been doing up until now to survive, maybe hurting others or using drugs or alcohol, how many of those values will you have to violate?

BARRIERS TO HEALTHY CONNECTIONS

Scientists have discovered that when we are cut off from others, our brains suffer. We tend to be angrier and depressed, use more drugs or alcohol, and feel sicker in general when we are isolated from others. We become better people when we are connected to others. We reach our full potential when we are connected to others who truly care about us.

What are some of the things that get in the way of building strong and caring relationships?

What are some things you can do to break those barriers?

OTHER WAYS WE COMMUNICATE

When we have trouble understanding what another person is feeling, we have trouble connecting. Things a person doesn't say out loud that give us some clues are called "nonverbal communication." These include a person's facial expressions, body language, and tone and volume of voice.

Effective communication also applies to listening when someone else is talking. Here are some possible strategies that help people to feel listened to:

- Maintaining eye contact
- Nodding your head
- Clearly giving the speaker your full attention

- Leaning slightly toward the speaker to indicate your interest
- Not interrupting
- Not making faces or gestures (such as crossing your arms) that indicate boredom or disagreement
- Not looking at your watch
- Silencing your cell phone and putting it away

Can you think of any other things to add to this list?

What are some other things you want to remember about nonverbal communication?

FOUR COMMUNICATION STYLES

There are four different styles of communicating that most of us use.

Passive

This style includes apologizing without expressing our ideas, feelings, or needs; using a hesitant voice; using poor eye contact; slouching; and letting others make decisions for us. An example: "I thought that, maybe, um, you could . . . ." Passive communication also is used when we do nothing or agree to do something that we really don't want to do. We may believe that we are being treated unfairly but we don't say anything. We may see something happening that is wrong and not do anything. Passive communicators seek to avoid conflict at all costs. We give up our wants and needs in order to temporarily keep the peace.

Passive-Aggressive

This style is about trying to get people to do what you want by being indirect or using disguised resistance, stalling, and/or stubbornness. An example: "I don't care if you go. I'll just sit home alone!" A passive-aggressive response is often the most confusing form of communication. We may say we agree with a request or an opinion and then walk away meaning to do something else entirely. An example is agreeing to help people even if we don't really want to and thinking that they should have done it themselves. Then we show up late and do a poor job of helping—maybe acting angry while we do it. We give a mixed message because we don't want to cause any problems, but our attitude causes a problem anyway.

Aggressive

This includes bossing people around, acting in a way that says other people's ideas and opinions don't matter, talking in a loud and demanding voice, staring down the other person, and having clenched hands and a threatening posture. Here are some examples: "You idiot! What were you thinking?" and "You'd better not do that anymore or you'll be really sorry." This can be a dangerous form of communication. If we are aggressive communicators, we are going to be "right" and get our way no matter if we hurt others. We are aggressive communicators when we interrupt, yell, blame, threaten, and even become violent with others. Aggression often gives us a short-term reward, because other people become afraid and back down. But the long-term price is that our relationships with others are hurt and may never be fully repaired.

Assertive

This form of communication is our goal. When we practice assertiveness, we use direct, clear, and honest communication and a voice that is firm but respectful. We make eye contact without staring and keep our hands and bodies relaxed. We clearly state what we want and need. Here are some examples: "I need you to tell me what's going on so that I can understand what you need" and "I cannot help you on Friday but I will be glad to do it on Saturday, if that works for you." Assertive communicators respect their own needs and boundaries and also those of the other persons.

Please make some notes about your typical communication styles here.

PRACTICING COMMUNICATION STYLES

How does it feel to be assertive?

What are some benefits of using an assertive communication style?

If you were to get better at an assertive communication style, how might that affect different relationships in your life? How might it help you to reach your goals?

PROGRESSIVE MUSCLE RELAXATION

1. Get comfortable in your seat or lying down.
2. Close your eyes or focus your eyes on a spot on the floor in front of you.
3. Take a few moments to relax, breathing in and out in slow, deep breaths.
4. Now focus your attention on your feet. Take a moment to focus on the way your feet feel.
5. Slowly tense the muscles in your feet, squeezing them as tightly as you can. Hold this for a count of ten.
6. Relax your feet. Focus on the tension flowing away and the way your feet feel relaxed.
7. Stay in this relaxed state for a moment, breathing slowly and deeply.
8. Now tense the muscles in your calves. Hold this for a count of ten.
9. Relax your calves. Feel the tension flowing away. Breathe slowly and deeply.
10. Now tense the muscles in your thighs. Hold them tight for a count of ten.
11. Relax the muscles in your thighs. Feel the tension flow away. Breathe slowly and deeply.
12. Tense the muscles in your hips and buttocks. Hold this for a count of ten.
13. Now relax your hips and buttocks. Feel the tension flowing out. Keep breathing.
14. Tense the muscles in your abdomen. Hold them tight for a count of ten.
15. Relax your abdomen. Feel the tension flowing out. Breathe.
16. Now tense up your chest muscles. Hold this for a count of ten.
17. Relax your chest muscles. Let the tension flow out. Breathe.

18. Tense up your back muscles. Hold this while you count to ten.

19. Relax your back. Feel the tension oozing out. Breathe.

20. Now tense the muscles in your arms and hands. Hold them tight for a count of ten.

21. Relax your arms and hands. Let the tension flow out. Breathe.

22. Tense the muscles in your neck and shoulders. Hold them tight while you count to ten.

23. Relax your neck and shoulders. Let the tension flow out of them while you breathe slowly and deeply.

24. Tense the muscles in your face. Hold for a count of ten.

25. Relax your facial muscles. Breathe slowly and deeply.

26. Now open your eyes.

- -

REFLECTION

Reflect on what was meaningful to you in this session and what you want to remember. Then write or draw about it here.

1. Please review your Word Cloud on page 5. Now that you've learned more about connecting with others, are there any words you might want to add to or remove from your Word Cloud? If you feel like it, you can share any changes you've made during our next session.

2. Teach someone you feel comfortable with two of the grounding activities you've learned and ask the person about their experience with them. Record your findings in the space provided.

Abuse and Conflict

THIS SESSION

In this session, you learn about the different types of abuse in relationships and you are given lists of resources for people who experience abuse. You practice more grounding or self-mastery techniques that you can use when you are stressed or in times of conflict. You also learn about and practice useful conflict-resolution techniques.

SQUARE BREATHING

1. Sit up straight in your chair.
2. Close your eyes or focus your eyes on a spot on the floor in front of you.
3. Breathe in to a count of four: one, two, three, four.
4. Hold your breath for a count of four: one, two, three, four.
5. Exhale to a count of four: one, two, three, four.
6. Hold the exhale for a count of four: one, two, three, four.
7. Repeat. Breathe in: one, two, three, four.
8. Hold the breath: one, two, three, four.
9. Exhale: one, two, three, four.
10. Hold the exhale: one, two, three, four.
11. Once again, this time, thinking to yourself that you are safe in this space.
12. Breathe in: one, two, three, four.
13. Hold the breath: one, two, three, four.
14. Exhale: one, two, three, four.
15. Hold the exhale: one, two, three, four.

16. Repeat the breathing one last time, while you give yourself permission to be open-minded.

17. Breathe in: one, two, three, four.

18. Hold the breath: one, two, three, four.

19. Exhale: one, two, three, four.

20. Hold the exhale: one, two, three, four.

ABUSIVE RELATIONSHIPS

Abusive relationships are the opposite of healthy connections, and abuse happens to many people in all walks of life.

Young people who experience abuse may think their experiences are "normal," may blame themselves, may just live with the pain of abuse, and may turn to alcohol or other drugs to numb their pain. They may remain silent because of threats made by their abusers. They may have been told that the abuse is their "fault" or they may be embarrassed about their experiences. You need to know that abuse is *never* the victim's fault.

All acts of abuse are ways the abuser tries to break down the victim's self-confidence and limit the victim's ability to act independently. It can leave the abused person feeling isolated and alone. Abuse is any behavior that threatens, intimidates, takes advantage of, exploits, or deliberately harms another person in some way or misuses trust. Abuse is a way of controlling, demeaning, or "punishing" another person. Abuse can take many forms. Some abuse is physical, some is psychological, some is verbal, and some is done by means of social media, such as cyberbullying and trashing. Even telling things about others without their permission or starting or continuing rumors about others is abusive behavior.

- *Emotional abuse* includes name calling, criticizing, bullying, belittling, humiliating a person publicly or privately or on social media, dead naming a trans person or intentionally using the wrong pronouns for a person, being possessive and/or extremely jealous, isolating a person from friends and family, withholding affection as a means of punishment, blaming, threatening, stalking, terrorizing, manipulating, playing mind games, controlling another's appearance, destroying a person's property or possessions, and threatening a person or those he or she loves with violence.

- *Cyber abuse*, also called cyberbullying, includes bullying or harassing others on cell phones or the internet—particularly on social media sites, in chat rooms, or by e-mail. It includes posting rumors, threats, or sexual remarks; posting someone's personal information; trolling; cyberstalking; and hate speech, including racial and ethnic slurs, and gay or trans bashing.

- *Physical abuse* includes pinching, pushing, fighting, slapping, shaking, spitting, hair pulling, kicking, choking, throwing things, holding down, biting, burning, threatening with a weapon, harassing to the point of physical illness, depriving of sleep, depriving of food or water, deliberately passing on a sexually transmitted disease, forcibly confining, and physically injuring in any other way.

- *Sexual abuse* ranges from psychological abuse to overt physical abuse. It includes raping, touching in unwanted or inappropriate ways, treating another as a sex object, forcing another to have sex in front of or with others, forcing another to engage in sadistic sexual acts, coercing another with threats of leaving the relationship or of telling people untruths if the person does not comply with the abuser, attempting to have intercourse with a person who is under the influence of alcohol or other drugs, blackmailing a person for sex, and making fun of a person because of the person's sex organs or sexual functioning.

Source: S. S. Covington. (2016). *Beyond Trauma: A Healing Journey for Women* (Rev. ed.). (pp. 262–264). Center City, MN: Hazelden.

Continuum of Sexual Abuse

Psychological Abuse   *Covert Abuse*   *Overt Abuse*

Psychological sexual abuse is subtle and may be hard to recognize. It could be a parent or other adult looking to a child for emotional comfort that has a sexualized tone, telling sexual jokes or using profanity around children, making personalized sexual remarks, and violating personal boundaries.

Covert sexual abuse includes reading or watching pornographic material with a child, "accidental" inappropriate touching, voyeurism, and ridiculing someone's sexual organs.

More overt abuse includes exhibitionism, fondling, French kissing, oral sex, and sexual penetration of an underage or unwilling partner.

You may want to make some notes here as a result of your group's discussion.

SOOTHING AND GROUNDING: SELF-MASTERY TECHNIQUES

Learning how to calm yourself and to relax when you have been bombarded by intense emotions is a valuable skill. You can experiment to find activities that work best for you.

Soothing Activities

- Taking long, deep breaths
- Listening to music
- Taking a long, hot shower or bath
- Taking a walk
- Thinking about a good memory
- Remembering a safe place that you find very soothing (perhaps the beach or mountains or a favorite room) and focusing on everything about it: the sounds, colors, shapes, objects, textures, and smells
- Thinking about people you care about and looking at photographs of them or imagine them smiling at you
- Thinking of your favorite animal, season, car, food, time of day, or television show
- Talking to a trusted friend
- Writing in a journal

- Reading

- Painting or drawing

- Writing down what you want to say to someone

- Saying kind statements to yourself, such as "You are a good person going through a hard time; you'll get through this"

- Say a coping statement, such as "I can handle this" or "This feeling will pass"

- Reciting the words to an inspiring song, quotation, or poem that makes you feel better

- Planning a safe treat for yourself, such as a piece of candy or a favorite food or a nice dinner

- Thinking of something you are looking forward to in the next week, such as spending time with a person you like

Is there anything you want to add to this list?

There are mental grounding techniques and physical grounding techniques. You can use mental grounding when, for some reason, you cannot use physical grounding. Grounding helps us be in the present, especially if we have experienced a trigger or activator that reminds us of a traumatic event.

Mental Grounding

- Describe your environment in detail using all your senses. For example, "The walls are white, there are five brown chairs, there is a wooden bookshelf against the wall." Describe objects, sounds, textures, colors, smells, shapes, numbers, and temperature. You can do this anywhere.

- Play a "categories" game with yourself. Try to think of "types of dogs," "musicians," "states that begin with 'A,'" "cars," "funny television shows," "writers," "sports stars," "songs," or "state capitals."

- Do an age progression. Sometimes when we are emotionally triggered, we may feel like we're younger, maybe even a little kid. If you are feeling younger than you actually are, then you may have regressed to a younger age. You can slowly work your way back up by saying "I'm now nine," "I'm now ten," "I'm now eleven," until you are back to your current age.

- Describe an everyday activity in great detail. For example, describe a meal that you can cook by going through all the steps. Or shooting a basketball or passing a football.

- Use an image: Glide along on skates away from your pain, change the television channel to get to a better show, think of a wall as a buffer between you and your pain.

- Say a safety statement, such as, "My name is _____; I am safe right now. I am in the present, not the past. I am located in _____; the date is _____."

- Read something, saying each word to yourself. Or read each letter backwards so that you focus on the letters and not the meanings of the words.

- Use humor. Think of something funny to jolt yourself out of your mood.

- Count to ten or say the alphabet very slowly.

- Repeat a favorite saying or poem to yourself over and over.

Physical Grounding

- Run cool or warm water over your hands.

- Grab tightly onto your chair as hard as you can.

- Touch various objects around you, such as a pen, keys, your clothing, the table, the walls. Notice textures, colors, materials, weight, and temperature. Compare objects you touch: Is one colder? Lighter?

- Dig your heels into the floor, literally "grounding" them. Notice the tension centered in your heels as you do this. Remind yourself that you are connected to the ground.

- Carry a grounding object in your pocket, such as a small rock, ring, piece of cloth, or something else that you can touch whenever you feel anxious or stressed.

- Jump up and down.
- Notice your body: the weight of your body in the chair, the feel of your back against the chair. Wiggle your toes. You are connected to the world.
- Stretch. Extend your fingers, arms, or legs as far as you can; roll your head around.
- Walk slowly, noticing each footstep, saying "left," and "right" with each step.
- Eat something and describe the flavors in detail to yourself.
- Focus on your breath, noticing each inhale and exhale. Repeat a pleasant word to yourself with each inhale (for example, a favorite color or a soothing word such as "safe" or "easy").

Is there anything you want to add to this list?

A PHYSICAL GROUNDING TECHNIQUE

1. Sit comfortably in a chair without slouching with your feet on the floor.
2. Notice how that feels. Notice your bottom sitting in the chair.
3. Notice the temperature of the room and how that feels.
4. Choose an object in the room and look at it.
5. Think of what it might feel like.
6. Pretend that you are examining it.
7. As you look, breathe slowly in and out.
8. Then bring your attention back to the present.

Grounding Tips

- Try to notice whether you do better with physical or mental grounding.
- Practice as often as possible, even when you don't "need" it, so that you'll know it by heart. Practicing helps to create new pathways in the brain so that what you are learning to do becomes easier.
- Practice faster. Speeding up the pace gets you focused on the outside world quickly.
- Create your own methods of grounding. Any method you make up may be worth much more than those you learn because it is yours.
- Start grounding early in a negative mood cycle. Start when the substance craving just starts or when you have just started to have a flashback or when you realize that you are becoming tense or stressed or agitated.

THE CONTAINER

You learned "The Container" technique in Session Three and practice it again in this session. Sometimes, sharing your feelings can be overwhelming or even dangerous. You may have an emotional reaction that you do not expect or that is more intense than you feel you can handle. It's important for you to be able to contain your feelings so that you can choose when and how to express yourself. This does not mean stuffing or ignoring your feelings; it means choosing when and how to express them safely and appropriately.

Here are some more tips for managing how you express your feelings.

Tips for Containing Feelings

1. Slow down or stop what you're doing.
2. Identify what you're feeling.

3. Name the feeling.

4. Notice where you feel it in your body.

5. Evaluate whether the intensity of the feeling matches the situation.

6. Consider what other factors may be contributing to your intense feeling. If the intensity does not match the situation, ask yourself how old you are as you have this feeing. It may belong to another time in your life.

7. Practice placing your feelings in your container.

YOGA

One time-honored way to help your mind and body to be in sync is to practice yoga. Yoga helps you to be "mindful" by focusing on your deliberate bodily movements. It is a centuries-old practice and it isn't just for moms and Asian monks!

You will find selected yoga poses in Appendix 3 of this workbook, starting on page 181.

CONFLICT RESOLUTION: THE STARE TECHNIQUE

Conflict is a normal part of what happens when two or more people share the same space. Most of us don't have too much trouble communicating when we are talking about things we see as positive, but we may have problems when we are trying to avoid conflict or resolve conflict. We may not have been taught healthy ways of dealing with conflict. We may have learned by watching others to be aggressive or to avoid conflict, but being aggressive or avoiding conflict will lead to problems in a relationship. Sometimes it leads to more serious consequences, such as physical harm and legal problems. If you combine aggression with alcohol and other drugs, a person's behavior is much more unpredictable and hurtful.

Conflict doesn't have to mean fighting. Conflict can be thought of as simply a difference in the way each person thinks or feels about something. When we solve a conflict, it can help us build a stronger and closer relationship.

STARE Conflict-Resolution Guide

*S*tart positively. Ask for a chance to speak. Say something positive about your relationship (maybe express something you appreciate about the person or about your relationship together).

*T*ell the person how you're feeling about what happened or what you saw, not about that person personally. No attacking. No labeling. No criticizing. No judging. No blaming. No accusing. No buts.

*A*sk for a solution. We don't want to be ordered about, so we shouldn't order others to change their behaviors. Instead, we want to work together toward a solution, so we ASK the person for ideas.

(Pause and wait for the other person to tell you what that person heard you say. The other person repeats what was heard and offers a solution. If you both agree on the solution, continue to **R**.)

*R*eview the solution. We want to make sure we haven't wasted time simply talking about the issue. We want to make sure both persons feel heard and validated. Then we commit to working on the solution we identified together.

*E*nd positively. Thank each other for being willing to talk about and work on the issue. Express appreciation for each other. Set a time in the future when you'll check on the progress you've made and CELEBRATE what you've done well together!

Source: S. S. Covington & R. A. Rodriguez. (2016). *Exploring Trauma: A Brief Intervention for Men* (p. 143). Center City, MN: Hazelden.

The **S** reminds us to *start* positively.

The **T** reminds us to *tell* the other person how we feel without attacking, labeling, criticizing, judging, blaming, or accusing. We use "I" statements; that means we describe how we're feeling or what we're thinking without presuming that we know what the other person meant when that person did something or said something.

The **A** reminds us to *ask* for a solution. We aren't trying to change the other person; we want that person's help in resolving the conflict.

Notice that there is a pause there after the A. This is so that the other person can *reflect* back to us what that person heard us communicate. That means trying to repeat, word for word, what we just said.

The **R** reminds us to *review* the solution once we've come up with one and to make a commitment to follow through.

The **E** reminds us to *end* positively, to thank each other, and to show appreciation for each other. This step makes us feel good about what we've just accomplished.

REFLECTION

Reflect on what was meaningful to you in this session and what you want to remember. Then write or draw about it here.

BETWEEN-SESSIONS ACTIVITY

1. Practice some of the grounding and self-soothing activities you learned in this session. Make some notes about which ones worked best for you.

2. Do some experimenting with the differences between mental grounding and physical grounding. Notice how you feel after doing each type. Make some notes about this.

Mothers

THIS SESSION

Most of us form opinions about women by seeing how our mothers—or people such as grandmothers, aunts, older sisters, or foster mothers who played the roles of our mothers—act and how they are treated by their husbands or boyfriends or partners. We also learn about women in our interactions with sisters and other girls. The media also gives us messages about females. In this session, you explore how your view of your mother or mother substitute affects your views of girls and women. We may not realize that some of our behavior toward girls and women is potentially oppressive or abusive.

Many people still think of women only as caregivers, whose work is valued less and who are expected to submit to the will of men. In this session, you also look at some limiting ways that society has viewed women.

Finally, the session may help you to see your mother or mother substitute as a real person—a multidimensional, human being with challenges just like everybody else. This may increase your understanding of your mother.

BREATHING

There may be times when we are stressed out or angry but we can't leave or we are restricted to sitting. During these times, deep breathing may be all we can do to ground and calm ourselves, so it's important to practice.

1. Sit comfortably in your chair without slouching.
2. Breathe in and silently count to four. One, two, three, four.
3. Hold your breath. One, two, three, four.

4. Breathe out while counting to four. One, two, three, four.

5. Hold your breath again. One, two, three, four.

6. Repeat this four more times.

WHAT DO MOTHERS DO?

1. What are mothers "supposed" to do? You may want to make some notes here about your group's discussion.

_____

_____

_____

_____

_____

_____

_____

2. What happens when the mom has a problem with alcohol or drugs and can't do the things on the first list?

_____

_____

_____

_____

_____

_____

_____

MY MOM

1. Think back to when you were a little kid. What was your relationship with your mother (or the person who played the role of your mother) like then?

2. If your mother is still alive, how would you describe your relationship with her now? If she is not alive, how do you hold on to the memory of your mother?

3. What do you know about your mother's life when she was a child, a teenager, and an adult?

4. What did you learn about being masculine from your mother?

REFLECTION

Reflect on what was meaningful to you in this session and what you want to remember. Then write or draw about it here.

BETWEEN-SESSIONS ACTIVITY

Take a few minutes to answer the following questions.

1. How has what you learned about mother myths changed the way you might think or feel about your mother?

2. Do you think that women typically have had the same chance to make their dreams come true as men have?

3. If you could, what would you do to change that?

_____

_____

_____

_____

_____

_____

_____

Please draw your container here. It can be the same or different than the one you drew before in Session Three, page 25.

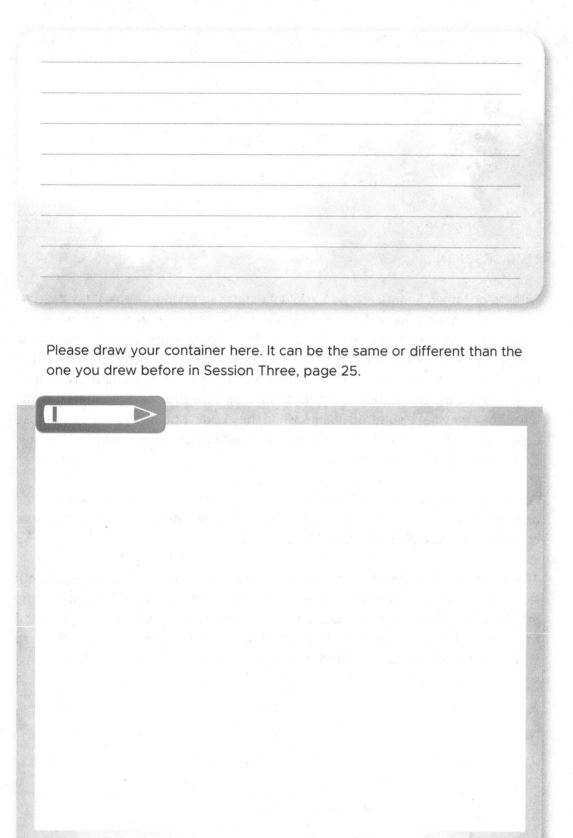

Fathers

THIS SESSION

Fathers or father figures are powerful influences in young peoples' lives. Some fathers are great. Some fathers are physically or emotionally absent. Some fathers or other men in the household may be abusive. Many young people have conflicting feelings about the grown men in their lives and about the messages they received about what it means to be a man or to be masculine. They may have been taught that they need to be strong, powerful, and in control all the time. They may have suffered shame when they could not always live up to those unrealistic expectations. They may have difficulty expressing anger as it relates to their experiences with their fathers.

For those who do not identify with a binary gender or gender as an idea, the pressure to be or act a certain way can be very challenging. When that pressure comes from our fathers, it can feel inescapable.

This session is designed to help you to think about the life experiences of your father (or a man who played the role of a father in your life) and the problems he may have faced. You explore the myths about fatherhood and the sense of failure that many fathers have as a result of their belief in these myths. You may begin to view your father as a whole person with his own hopes, dreams, and flaws.

WHAT DO FATHERS DO?

1. What are fathers "supposed" to do? You may want to make some notes here about your group's discussion.

2. How do men typically feel when they are expected to take care of children and show they how they feel?

3. How do children feel when their fathers are not able to show them how they feel?

_____

_____

_____

_____

_____

_____

_____

_____

_____

4. How do children feel when their fathers are not in their lives for some reason?

_____

_____

_____

_____

_____

_____

_____

_____

5. What happens when the dad has a problem with alcohol or other drugs and can't do the things on our first list?

_____
_____
_____
_____
_____
_____
_____
_____
_____

MY DAD

1. Think back to when you were little. What was your relationship with your father figure like at that time?

_____
_____
_____
_____
_____
_____
_____
_____

2. If your father is still alive, how would you describe your relationship with him now?

3. What do you know about your father's life when he was a child and a teenager?

4. Do you know what your father's goals were when he was younger? Was he able to achieve them?

5. What did you learn about being masculine from your father? (If you are trans or nonbinary or nonconforming, you may want to write about how this has affected your relationship with your dad.)

LETTER TO MY DAD

REFLECTION

Reflect on what was meaningful to you in this session and what you want to remember. Then write or draw about it here.

BETWEEN-SESSIONS ACTIVITY

Between now and the next session, review the list of self-mastery and grounding activities beginning on page 10. Choose one or two that you would feel comfortable leading the group through. Practice with someone you trust. You will be asked to volunteer to lead the Self-Mastery activity to open and close the next session.

Relationships

Friendship

THIS SESSION

The idea that deep and intimate relationships, especially with our peers, are not valuable to us is a myth. It is simply not true. However, if you have lived around lots of conflict and other challenges, you may not trust others enough to fully engage in a relationship or to enter one only if you believe that you have the upper hand.

This session highlights the importance of forming deeper relationships. It helps you to understand the different ways in which people interact with one another, how power can be a barrier to relationships, and the characteristics of effective relationships. It also helps you to examine how you engage in relationships and to think about the kind of friend you want to have and to be.

POWER AND RELATIONSHIPS

A lot of us have been taught to think that if we have power over someone or something, we can feel safe. This may work for us in the short term, but if we look at relationships this way, it will probably make them shallow and one-sided.

The communication styles of passive, aggressive, passive-aggressive, and assertive can be related to the three ways people behave in relationships.

This represents a relationship between two people. Like the aggressive or passive style, this relationship is "leveraged." It is sometimes called a "one-up" relationship, meaning that the person on the left has all the power in the relationship and the person on the right is passive or is "one down."

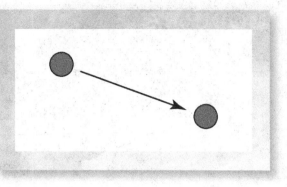

This represents a one-up relationship that is leveraged the other way. Here the person on the right has all the power and the one on the left is passive or one down.

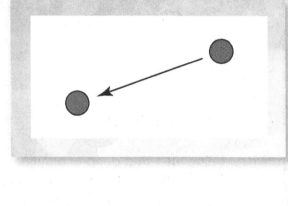

This represents a relationship that is similar to the assertive communication style. Each person has an equal amount of power in the relationship. No one is dominating the other.

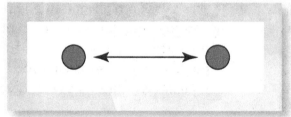

In the following space, please list one or two close friendships that you have. You can include romantic partners if you wish. You will always be the circle on the left, and your friend will be the circle on the right.

Place an arrow between the names to represent the relationship. Which way is it leveraged? Are you one-up, one-down, or equal? Do this for each relationship. You will have two or three minutes for this part of the activity.

Example:

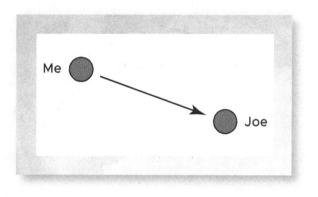

DISCUSSION QUESTIONS

1. Who has the power in your relationship?

2. Do you compete in your relationship?

3. How does that affect your friendship?

4. What would the other person say about your friendship?

5. Why do you think your friendship turned out that way?

6. What would you do differently if you could?

THE RELATIONSHIP WHEEL

The foundation, or core, of any healthy relationship is respect, mutuality, and compassion.

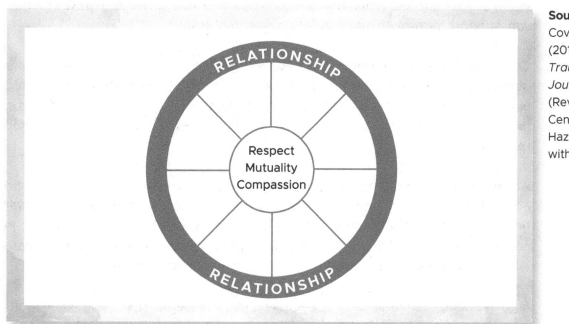

Source: S. S. Covington. (2016). *Beyond Trauma: A Healing Journey for Women* (Rev. ed.). (p. 377). Center City, MN: Hazelden. Reprinted with permission.

Respect is something that grows when we see the other person act with integrity. We earn respect when we're willing to do the right thing, even when it's hard. We learn to respect others when we see how they behave and the good decisions they make when the choices are difficult.

Mutuality means you are both working hard on the relationship. Each person has a willingness and desire to really see the other person as well as to be seen, to hear the other as well as to be heard, and to be vulnerable as well as to respect the other's vulnerability. Mutuality also means there's an awareness of the "we," not a sole focus on two individuals.

Compassion is similar to empathy, but it goes a little deeper. Empathy is understanding another's feelings and being able to feel *with* the person. When we're compassionate, we give of ourselves to be with the other person emotionally. When we're compassionate, we want to help end another person's suffering.

CHARACTERISTICS OF EFFECTIVE RELATIONSHIPS

Similarities. This means that you sort of feel and think the same most times. It means that you and the other person have shared interests, that you find most of the same things important and fun. It also means that you tend to have the same vision of your futures. When one of you is trying to stay sober and grow as a person, support for growth and sobriety is also important.

Compatible Values. A lot of young people don't talk about values when they are getting to know each other. As a relationship grows, values always come into play. But talking about values isn't enough. A person's *real* values are reflected in how the person lives and behaves. Learning about people's values by observation takes time.

Ability to Deal with Change. Life is always changing, and we have to change and adapt. People's needs and the ways in which they look at life also change over time. In any close relationship, when a person's needs change, the change can cause a major conflict. So, dealing with change in a respectful and compassionate way is very important if you want to keep the relationship going.

Firm Personal Boundaries. People have physical, emotional, and intellectual boundaries that can be violated in different ways. If you want a strong relationship, you have to know when and how to set clear limits. Each person should also accept and honor the boundaries and limits set by the other person.

Healthy Sexual Expression. Sexuality is a powerful form of communication. It's important for partners to feel free to express their sensuality and sexuality with each other. Safety is also an important element of healthy sexuality. No one should be forced to do anything sexually that they are not comfortable doing. Sexuality is healthy when both partners feel good about it.

Shared Quality Time. Quality time is "at ease" time—open ended, without built-in schedules or endings. It means that the two people in the relationship are willingly being open, accepting whatever comes.

Friendship. Friendship is the cornerstone of any relationship. Even in a romantic relationship, it's hard to imagine that relationship evolving into a healthy, successful, loving partnership without a strong element of friendship.

Clear Communication. Good communication is important in all human relationships. It's especially important to be clear about the intent behind a message. When you aren't aware of your motives or aren't clear about your intent when speaking, and when your words or body language don't fit the situation, the result is a mixed message, which is confusing to the listener. Clear communication can reduce conflict by eliminating needless misunderstandings and resentments.

Effective Conflict Resolution. The closer the love relationship, the more individual differences become obvious and the greater the possibility of conflict. Differences between two people are to be expected, and they can be wonderful assets in a relationship, but they also can create challenges, particularly if there's no open communication and there are poor negotiation skills. Especially when one is angry, it's important to speak with "I" statements that express your thoughts and feelings, rather than "you" statements that blame the other person or attribute motives or feelings to the other person. "I" statements explain where you're coming from and help the other person understand what's going on with you. "You" statements can be misinterpretations of the other person's motives, feelings, or behaviors, and they often generate defensiveness and a lack of willingness to negotiate.

Effective Negotiation. Successful negotiation occurs when two people find a solution that both of them can live with. It's an effective way to resolve conflict. One way to think about negotiation is in terms of needs and wants. Needs are essential things a person has to have and wants are preferences. In a relationship, one person's needs should have priority over the other person's wants. Another way to negotiate is to think about what the relationship needs in order to survive and grow, rather than what each individual may need or want.

These aspects of healthy relationships are not limited to romantic love partnerships. They're important in all relationships that hold the promise of openness and intimacy, including close friendships.

REFLECTION

Reflect on what was meaningful to you in this session and what you want to remember. Then write or draw about it here.

BETWEEN-SESSIONS ACTIVITY

Sometime between now and the next session, make a list of the qualities that you bring to your friendships. Make a list of the things you have to work on to improve your friendships. Be sure to include what would be helpful to you as you try to improve. This topic will be reviewed in your next session.

Gender and Sexuality

THIS SESSION

Sexuality is more than physical sexual behavior. Sexuality involves our physical, emotional, social, and spiritual selves. Your sexuality includes your perceptions and feelings about yourself and your perceptions and feelings about others. It involves how you act and with whom you act. So, sexuality is not just about having sex; it involves many aspects of who you are.

This session is designed to help you become more comfortable talking about sex and sexuality. It includes a discussion of risky and harmful sexual behaviors. It explains the differences among sex, gender, gender expression, and sexual orientation. Finally, it encourages you to think of the qualities you want in a partner and the attributes you may want to develop in order to attract your ideal partner.

DATING AND SEXUALITY

1. Where did you learn most of what you know about sex—from someone in your family, from a class at school, from your friends, on your own, or somewhere else?

_____

_____

_____

_____

_____

_____

_____

_____

_____

2. Are there different expectations for those raised as girls and for those raised as boys when it comes to sex?

_____

_____

_____

_____

_____

_____

3. What kind of messages are there about girls who have sex?

_____
_____
_____
_____
_____
_____
_____
_____
_____

4. Have you ever decided not to see someone because the person had had sex with someone else?

_____
_____
_____
_____
_____
_____
_____
_____

5. What kind of messages are there about boys who have sex? What if they don't have sex?

_____
_____
_____
_____
_____
_____
_____
_____

6. Who can you talk to about sex in an honest and open way?

_____
_____
_____
_____
_____
_____
_____
_____

7. How does it feel to talk about sex in a group like this with other young people?

_____

_____

_____

_____

_____

_____

_____

_____

_____

_____

_____

_____

_____

Risky and Harmful Sexual Behaviors

- Taking advantage of a drunk or drugged partner
- Date rape
- Dishonest or manipulative actions to have sex
- Infidelity, having affairs
- Unprotected sex
- Other risky sexual behaviors
- Neglecting a partner's needs or desires
- Using drugs to enhance sexual experiences
- Using alcohol or other drugs to give oneself permission to act out sexually
- Compulsive sexual behavior
- Going along with a peer group's behavior in violation of personal values
- Avoiding intimacy other than physical interaction
- Avoiding physical relationships

GENDER IDENTITY AND SEXUAL ORIENTATION

Other complex aspects of sexuality are "gender identity" and "sexual orientation." Adolescence is a time of exploring one's sexual self and beginning to figure out who one is as a person and whom one is attracted to sexually. It is very normal for some young people to be curious about their sexuality at this stage of life. It is also normal to confuse sexual identity with gender.

- One's "sex" is usually is determined or assigned at birth, primarily based on the most obvious sex organs.
- One's "gender identity" is the gender a person feels, regardless of which sex the person was assigned at birth by a doctor or parents. Gender identity can be expressed with terms such as "male," "female," "intersex," "nonbinary," "transgender," "genderqueer," and more.
- "Gender expression" is how people express their gender by the clothing they wear, the way they wear their hair, the way they use makeup and accessories, their vocal inflection, and their body language. There may be degrees of masculinity and/or femininity in gender expression.
- "Cisgender" describes persons whose gender identity and expression match the sex assigned at birth.
- "Intersex" is a person with sex organs that can't be easily recognized as male or female.
- "Transgender" describes a person who identifies as a sex other than that which was assigned at birth.
- "Sexual orientation" is different from gender identity. It is used to describe the sex of those to whom a person is physically attracted, whether it is persons of the same sex, the opposite sex, or both sexes.

  - A "straight" or "heterosexual" person is someone who is attracted to persons of the opposite sex.
  - "Homosexual" is a term used to describe someone who is physically attracted to persons of the same sex. A homosexual male often is referred to as "gay," and a homosexual female often is referred to as "lesbian."
  - "Bisexual" is a term used to describe someone who is physically attracted to persons of both sexes.

Appendix 4 contains a more complete list of terms related to gender identity and sexual orientation.

MASCULINITY AND FEMININITY

All people have some qualities generally regarded as male and some regarded as female. However, many people raised as boys are taught early on to ignore, dislike, and hide the feminine parts of themselves. This is reinforced by being teased, mocked, humiliated, and even physically harmed when showing traits such as tenderness, compassion, an interest in the arts, and so on. However, when we deny the feminine parts of ourselves, we are experiencing relationships only half as deeply as we might.

MY IDEAL PARTNER

In the space below, please list characteristics of your ideal partner. What qualities does this partner have to have? What about looks? List *everything* you want this partner to have in order to attract you.

Now please list the qualities that you have that will attract your ideal partner.

REFLECTION

Reflect on what was meaningful to you in this session and what you want to remember. Then write or draw about it here.

BETWEEN-SESSIONS ACTIVITY

Between now and the next session, consider some questions you may have about sex, sexuality, gender, gender expression, and sexual orientation. Make a list of questions in the space below. We can review them during our next session.

You can write your questions here. In the next session, you can write them on a separate sheet of paper that you can hand in anonymously. There will be a place for you to put these during the next session.

Barriers to Healthy Relationships

THIS SESSION

This session explores barriers that exist in establishing and maintaining healthy, supportive relationships. Supportive relationships are those that help us to expand and grow. They help us to feel better about ourselves without hurting other people. Supportive relationships help us to see ourselves and others better. They help us to appreciate our self-worth, because others treat us as if we are worthwhile.

A relationship that is not supportive or is abusive makes a person feel confused and not connected. Such relationships tear people down and lead them away from accomplishing their goals and dreams.

This session can help you to understand the effects of privilege, power, control, violence, and abuse on your present and future relationships and helps you to identify alternatives to ineffective relationship behaviors.

It also helps you to look at your relationships in terms of those that lead to where you want to go and those that lead you away from your goals. Then you can start making wise choices about relationships. The session also provides guidance on ending relationships.

TEEN EQUALITY WHEEL

The Teen Equality Wheel shows ways in which you can build more equality into your relationships. You probably will notice that there are a lot of the elements you used in your Ideal Friend collage.

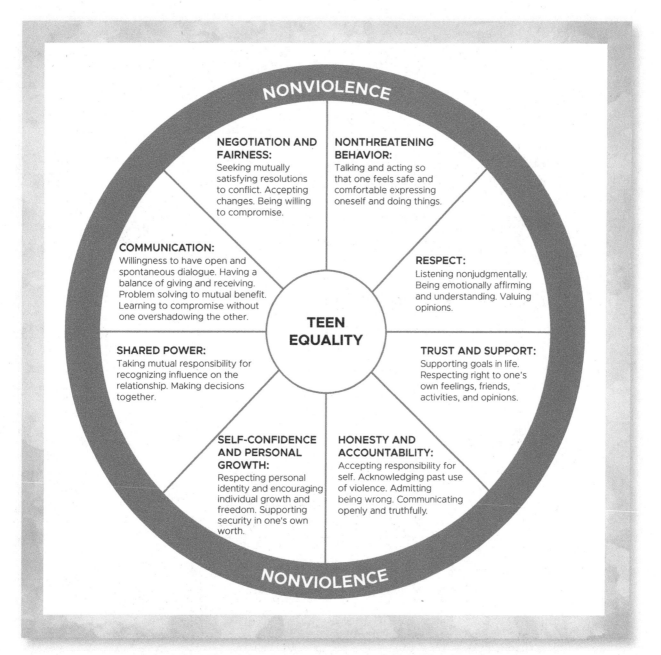

Source: Produced and distributed by National Center on Domestic and Sexual Violence www.ncdsv.org, Austin, TX. Adapted from Domestic Abuse Intervention Project, www.theduluthmodel.org/, Duluth, MN.

1. Have you had relationships that included all the elements on the wheel?

_____

_____

_____

_____

_____

_____

_____

_____

2. If not, what did that feel like?

_____

_____

_____

_____

_____

_____

_____

_____

3. Which elements might have been missing from your relationships?

_____
_____
_____
_____
_____
_____
_____
_____
_____
_____

4. What did that feel like?

_____
_____
_____
_____
_____
_____
_____
_____
_____

5. How do you think it would feel to have all these elements present in your relationships?

_____

_____

_____

_____

_____

_____

_____

_____

_____

6. What are you willing to do to make that possible?

_____

_____

_____

_____

_____

_____

_____

CONTROL AND ABUSE

It's natural to want to control our environment and the situations we are in. We think that having control means that we can feel safe and secure. However, when we control others to the extent that it hurts or injures them; when we mistreat, wrongfully harm, or violate their physical selves or their emotional boundaries; when we lie or mislead or break their trust; then our attempts to control become abuse.

You may have witnessed abuse or have been abused. Many times, if we were abused as children, we may think it happens to everyone. This could make us more likely to abuse others. Furthermore, people who experience abuse are more likely to use and develop problems with alcohol and other drugs.

Women, girls, and people in the LGBTQI community generally experience more abuse than others in our society. They may have to keep the abuse secret. They may experience shame and loneliness and may even blame themselves for the abuse.

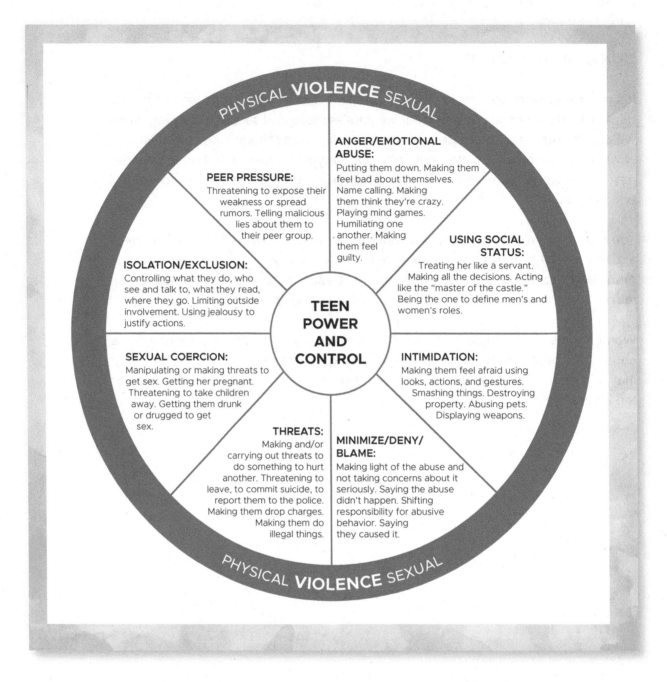

TEEN POWER AND CONTROL

ANGER/EMOTIONAL ABUSE: Putting them down. Making them feel bad about themselves. Name calling. Making them think they're crazy. Playing mind games. Humiliating one another. Making them feel guilty.

USING SOCIAL STATUS: Treating her like a servant. Making all the decisions. Acting like the "master of the castle." Being the one to define men's and women's roles.

INTIMIDATION: Making them feel afraid using looks, actions, and gestures. Smashing things. Destroying property. Abusing pets. Displaying weapons.

MINIMIZE/DENY/BLAME: Making light of the abuse and not taking concerns about it seriously. Saying the abuse didn't happen. Shifting responsibility for abusive behavior. Saying they caused it.

THREATS: Making and/or carrying out threats to do something to hurt another. Threatening to leave, to commit suicide, to report them to the police. Making them drop charges. Making them do illegal things.

SEXUAL COERCION: Manipulating or making threats to get sex. Getting her pregnant. Threatening to take children away. Getting them drunk or drugged to get sex.

ISOLATION/EXCLUSION: Controlling what they do, who see and talk to, what they read, where they go. Limiting outside involvement. Using jealousy to justify actions.

PEER PRESSURE: Threatening to expose their weakness or spread rumors. Telling malicious lies about them to their peer group.

PHYSICAL VIOLENCE SEXUAL

Source: Produced and distributed by National Center on Domestic and Sexual Violence www.ncdsv.org, Austin, TX. Adapted from Domestic Abuse Intervention Project, www.theduluthmodel.org, Duluth, MN.

1. Without giving names, do you know of someone—maybe a friend—who treats a partner this way?

2. In what ways has abuse touched your life or the life of someone you care about?

3. How have you seen others numb the pain of abuse?

_____

_____

_____

_____

_____

_____

_____

_____

_____

4. What have you tried to do when you saw these things happen?

_____

_____

_____

_____

_____

_____

_____

_____

5. What worked? What didn't work?

_____
_____
_____
_____
_____
_____
_____
_____
_____

6. What advice would you give a young person who is abusing their partner?

_____
_____
_____
_____
_____
_____
_____
_____

7. What advice would you give a young person who is being abused by their partner?

Remember the list you got in Session Six of national and local resources that can help people who have been involved in abusive relationships or who witness abuse in relationships. You can look at that list again if this session brings up something that you want to get help with. You also can talk to your facilitator privately to get additional support.

SUPPORTIVE RELATIONSHIPS

1. How has a person in your past showed you support?

2. What kind of support has it been difficult for you to ask for? Why?

3. What kind of support has it been easier for you to ask for?

_____

_____

_____

_____

_____

_____

_____

_____

_____

_____

_____

SAMPLE RELATIONSHIP MAP

A Relationship Map is divided into three parts: past, present, and future. It shows your relationships to people in your past and present. It also shows relationships you are considering in the future.

In the following sample, notice the different types of lines in the key at the bottom titled "Quality of Relationship." On your Relationship Map:

- Use a solid line to show relationships that you want to keep.
- Use a broken line with an arrow to show relationships that you want to start.
- Use a line with cross strokes to show relationships that you are ending or planning to end, perhaps because they are not supportive.

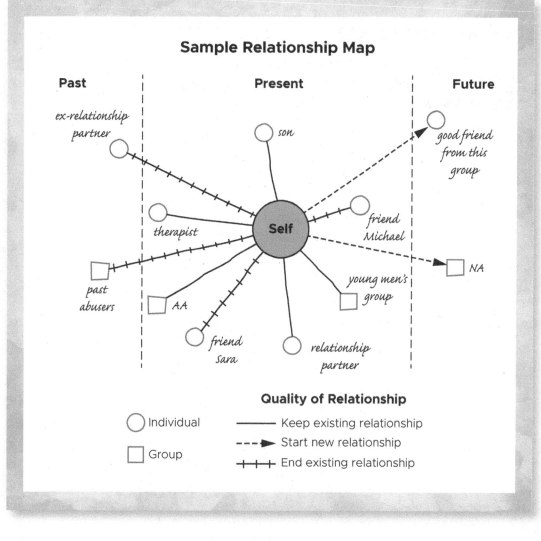

Sample Relationship Map

Past | Present | Future

ex-relationship partner

son

good friend from this group

therapist

Self

friend Michael

past abusers

AA

young men's group

NA

friend Sara

relationship partner

Quality of Relationship

◯ Individual — Keep existing relationship

▢ Group --- ▶ Start new relationship

+++ End existing relationship

Source: S. S. Covington. (2019). *Helping Women Recover* (Rev. ed.). (p. 442). San Francisco, CA: Jossey-Bass. Copyright 1999, rev. 2008 and 2019 by S. Covington. This material is used by permission of John Wiley & Sons, Inc.

In this sample, the solid lines mean that the young man wants to keep the relationships with sons, therapist, AA group, peer support group, and present relationship partner.

The person also is considering starting a new relationship with someone from the peer support group and is thinking about starting to attend an NA group. These are shown in the future, so the lines are different.

This map also shows that the young man is ending relationships with an ex-relationship partner, people who have been abusive in the past, a friend named Sara—who continues to use alcohol—and a friend named Michael, who is in a gang. Notice that these lines are crossed.

YOUR RELATIONSHIP MAP

ENDING RELATIONSHIPS

If you have experienced violence or abuse in the past, you may have a hard time ending relationships in a healthy way. This would be even harder if you and the person you are trying to end the relationship with are old using buddies.

1. When you think about ending a relationship, what things come to mind?

_____

_____

_____

_____

_____

_____

_____

_____

2. How have you ended relationships in the past?

_____

_____

_____

_____

_____

_____

_____

_____

3. If you have done it well, how did you do it?

_____
_____
_____
_____
_____
_____
_____
_____
_____

4. What are some of your ideas for ending a relationship in a healthy and respectful way?

_____
_____
_____
_____
_____
_____
_____
_____
_____

Tips for Ending a Relationship

- Be direct and honest.

- Speak using "I" statements rather than "You" statements.

- Express the feelings you're experiencing in the present.

- Assume personal responsibility for change.

- Decide on the level of intimacy or contact you want with the person in the future.

- Act in a timely way and agree on a time for the change to happen. (Examples: "I won't be answering your text messages or calls after today." Or "I'll move out by next Friday.")

- Let the other person know what you appreciate about that person.

- Let the other person know what you appreciated about the relationship.

1. What do you need to do in order to get better at ending relationships in a healthy and respectful way?

2. Who in your life can help you in this area?

REFLECTION

Reflect on what was meaningful to you in this session and what you want to remember. Then write or draw about it here.

BETWEEN-SESSIONS ACTIVITY

Between now and the next session, take some time to review your Relationship Map. Ask yourself: How are these relationships helping me become the kind of person I want to be? If you find that you need to redefine or end a relationship, how are you going to do it? Will you need help in doing so? If so, who can help you? You may want to make some notes on the previous page and/or here.

Healthy Living

Our Bodies

THIS SESSION

Media images and messages about the ideal body affect all of us. About one-third of teenage boys use unhealthy methods to control their weight. Young people are taught early on that the ideal man is muscular, fit, has a full head of hair, and is handsome. If young people have negative perceptions of their bodies, they may try to offset their perceived shortcomings by exaggerating other aspects of themselves and even engage in self-destructive behaviors in attempts to cope. This session is designed to help you become more accepting of your body, no matter how it differs from someone else's "ideal."

Part of self-mastery is taking care of one's body, mind, and spirit. This session will help you to understand ways to take better care of your body. The session also explores the connection between your body and your emotions. Many young people, especially young men, have learned not to share their feelings and have been taught that displaying feelings (other than, perhaps, anger) is a weakness. Even then, they may struggle with how to express their anger effectively. In this session, you identify where you learned attitudes about expressing feelings and how these messages affect how you presently express feelings.

HEALTHY LIVING SCALE

Please take a few moments to show how often you do each of the following things. You can make an "X" or a circle on each line to indicate your response.

	Not at All	Just a Little	Pretty Much	Very Much
1. I keep up my physical appearance.				
2. I exercise regularly.				
3. I eat healthy meals.				
4. I get restful sleep.				
5. I complete tasks at work/school.				
6. I can adapt to change.				
7. I keep up my living space.				
8. I take constructive criticism well.				
9. I can accept praise.				
10. I laugh at funny things.				
11. I acknowledge my needs and feelings.				
12. I engage in new interests.				
13. I can relax without alcohol or drugs.				
14. I value myself.				

Source: S. S. Covington. (2019). *Helping Women Recover* (Rev. ed.). (p. 163). San Francisco, CA: Jossey-Bass. Copyright 1999, rev. 2008 and 2019 by S. Covington. This material is used by permission of John Wiley & Sons, Inc.

BODY IMAGE

As a result primarily of magazines, movies, television, advertising, and social media, many young people are not satisfied with their bodies. Your body is an essential part of who you are. If you don't like your body or are uncomfortable with the way it looks and feels, you will not like part of yourself. Learning to accept, like, and respect your body is a huge part of self-mastery.

On the next page are two outlines of a body. One represents the front of your body and one represents the back.

1. Use a "plus" symbol (+) to mark the parts that you like on your body.

2. Use a "minus" symbol (−) to mark the parts of your body you don't like or feel uncomfortable with.

3. Use a zero (0) to mark those parts of your body you feel neutral about.

You're not going to be asked to share this. It is meant to help you to become more aware of how you look at and feel about your body.

Source: Adapted from S. S. Covington, D. Griffin, & R. Dauer. (2011). *Helping Men Recover: A Program for Treating Addiction*. San Francisco: Jossey-Bass.

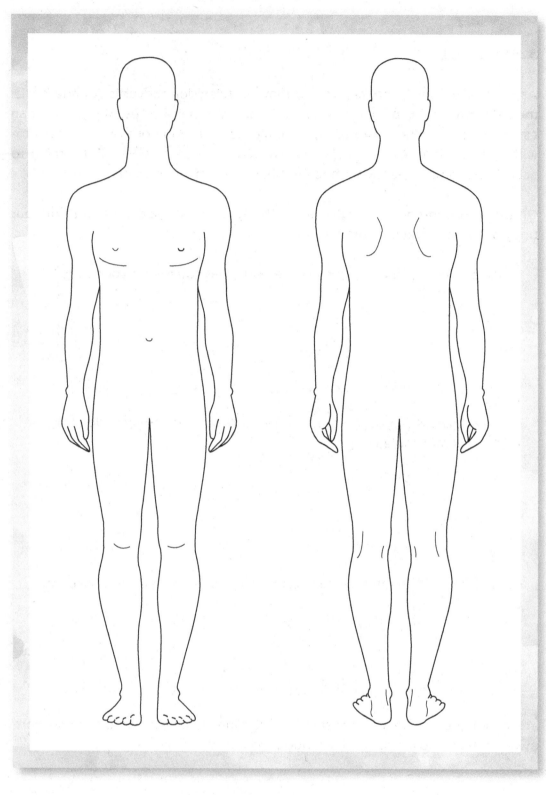

IMPROVING YOUR BODY IMAGE

1. Recognize that bodies come in all different sizes and shapes. There is no one "right" body size. Your body is not and should not be exactly like anyone else's. Try to see your body as an expression of your uniqueness and individuality.

2. Focus on the qualities in yourself that you like that are not related to appearance. Spend time developing these capacities, rather than letting your appearance define your identity and your worth.

3. Look critically at advertisements that push the "bodybuilding" message. Our culture emphasizes the V-shaped muscular body as the ideal for men. Magazines targeted at men tend to focus on articles and advertisements promoting weight lifting, bodybuilding, and muscle toning. Do you know people who have muscular, athletic bodies but who are not happy? Are there dangers in spending too much time focusing on your body? Consider giving up your goal of achieving the "perfect" body and work at accepting your body just the way it is.

4. Remember that your body size, shape, and weight do not determine your worth or your identity as a valuable person. In other words, you are not just your body. If you value masculine traits, expand your idea of "masculinity" to include qualities such as sensitivity, cooperation, caring, patience, having feelings, and being artistic. Some individuals may be muscular and athletic, but these qualities alone do not make someone a whole person or a good man.

5. Find friends who are not overly concerned with weight and appearance.

6. Be assertive with others who comment on your body. Let people know that comments about your physical appearance, either positive or negative, are not appreciated. Confront others who tease people about their bodies or who attack their masculinity by calling them names such as "sissy" and "wimp."

7. Demonstrate respect for people who possess body types or who display personality traits that do not meet the cultural standard for masculinity, that is, those who are slender, short, or overweight and those who dress colorfully or who enjoy activities such as dancing, cooking, and sewing.

8. Be aware of the negative messages you tell yourself about your appearance or body. Respond to negative self-talk with an affirmation. For example, if you start to think, "I look gross," substitute a positive affirmation, such as "I accept myself the way I am" or "I'm a worthwhile person."

9. Focus on the ways in which your body serves you and enables you to participate fully in life. In other words, appreciate how your body functions rather than obsessing about its appearance. For example, appreciate that your arms enable you to hold someone you love, your thighs enable you to run, the lungs in your chest enable you to breathe, and so on.

10. Aim for lifestyle mastery, rather than mastery over your body, weight, or appearance. Lifestyle mastery has to do with developing your unique gifts and potential, expressing yourself, developing meaningful relationships, learning how to solve problems, establishing goals, and contributing to life. View exercise and balanced eating as aspects of your overall approach to a life that emphasizes self-care.

Source: Adapted from T. Shiltz. (1997). Suggestions for Improving Body Image, Handout 7.1. *Eating Concerns Support Group Curriculum*. Greenfield, WI: Community Recovery Press.

HEALTHY AND UNHEALTHY EATING

There is a difference between body image and physical health. Body image is how we see and feel about our bodies. Physical health is about giving our bodies the food, exercise, and rest they need to keep us feeling good and functioning at our best. Some people may not feel good about their bodies even though they are physically healthy. Or they may think they look good but may not be taking good care of their bodies. They may be using alcohol or other drugs.

Nutrition is a major aspect of physical health. Food is necessary for life. It gives a body energy, builds muscle and bone, and keeps a person going. Healthy eating involves a balanced variety of foods throughout the day. For many of us, what and how we eat is tied to how we feel. Some of us eat to feel better when we feel bad. Some of us may eat or stop eating to feel that we are in control. Others may diet because they feel pressured to look a certain way.

Medical professionals used to think that only girls had eating disorders, but a lot of boys and men and gender diverse individuals also experience eating disorders that can damage their bodies and their senses of self. Here are some common eating disorders:

1. *Anorexia nervosa* is characterized by low body weight and behaviors that restrict food intake and/or eliminate food intake through actions such as vomiting and excessive exercise. People with anorexia nervosa have poor body images and are afraid of being overweight, even though they may be dangerously thin.

   I know someone who may be anorexic. ___Yes ___No

2. *Bulimia* is an eating disorder that is also characterized by an obsession with weight and body image. People with bulimia go on eating binges in which they eat a lot of food and feel out of control. They then force themselves to vomit, use laxatives, engage in excessive exercise, and/or fast to try to prevent any weight gain.

   I know someone who may be bulimic. ___Yes ___No

3. *Orthorexia nervosa* starts as an attempt to eat more healthfully, but the person becomes fixated on food quality and purity—with what and how much to eat. A rigid eating style develops into self-punishment if temptation wins (usually through stricter eating, fasts, and exercise). Self-esteem becomes based on the purity of one's diet and superiority to others in regard to food intake, and the diet can become too restrictive.

   I know someone who may have orthorexia nervosa. __Yes __No

4. *Compulsive overeating* is characterized by eating excessive amounts of food. Compulsive overeaters do not try to get rid of the food, as people with anorexia or bulimia do, but they often experience weight gain and the same negative feelings about their bodies.

   I know someone who may struggle with compulsive overeating. __Yes __No

Nutrition

Making healthy changes to our eating habits can be very difficult, but taking care of our bodies is an important step in self-mastery.

Shifting to healthier food and beverage choices means limiting calories from added sugars and saturated fats, reducing salt, drinking enough water, and eating from the five basic food groups every day. This helps us to get more nutrients, which is what the body needs for growth, maintenance, and repair. The six types of nutrients are water, vitamins, minerals, proteins, carbohydrates, and healthy fats.

The five basic food groups are vegetables, fruits, grains, protein, and dairy.

Vegetables: To get enough nutrients, we should choose a variety of vegetables every week:

- Leafy greens
- Red or orange vegetables
- Beans and peas (also part of the protein group)
- Starchy vegetables
- Other vegetables, such as eggplant and zucchini

Fruits: Eating whole fruits is much better than drinking juice. Juice contains more sugar, less fiber, and less nutrition. Some common fruits are apples, avocados, bananas, berries, cherries, grapes, kiwis, lemons, limes, mangos, melons, oranges, peaches, pears, pineapples, plums, strawberries, and watermelon.

Grains: There are two kinds of grains: whole grains and refined grains. Whole grains contain more protein and fiber than refined grains. Healthful whole grains include these:

- Quinoa
- Oats
- Brown rice
- Barley
- Buckwheat

Refined grains are processed. They are found in most breads (except whole-grain bread), most pancakes, waffles, baked goods such as pastries, and flour coatings on food.

Protein: All people should include nutrient-dense protein as part of their regular diets:

- Lean beef and pork (low fat or no fat)
- Chicken and turkey (not fried and with no skin)
- Fish (not fried)
- Beans, peas, and legumes (such as lentils)
- Tofu and other soy products

Dairy: Dairy products and fortified soy products are vital sources of calcium. A low-fat or 2% version is healthier. Low-fat dairy and soy products include these:

- Low-fat milk
- Ricotta or cottage cheese
- Yogurt

People who are lactose intolerant can choose lactose-free products, almond milk, oat milk, soy-based products such as soy milk, and so on.

Another aspect of nutrition is cutting out sugar. There's a lot of sugar in most sodas and other drinks, and in candy, desserts, and most prepared foods—including cereal and some other things that purport to be healthy.

Needless to say, not smoking and avoiding alcohol and other drugs is also very important. Taking care of our bodies also means getting enough sleep: seven or eight hours per night for most people. A lot of people take better care of their cars than they do of their bodies. But you can't trade your body in for a new model every few years!

EMOTIONAL WELLNESS

Tips for Emotional Wellness

1. *Tune in to your feelings.* This means being aware of when you have a feeling.

2. *Name the feeling.* How would you describe the feeling (for example: angry, sad, happy, frustrated, afraid)?

3. *Locate the feeling in your body.* Often, if you close your eyes and concentrate on the feeling, you will feel a sensation in your body, such as a tightness in your chest, a funny feeling in your stomach, tension in your neck or shoulders, or tension in your arms or hands.

4. *Express the feeling.* Say it out loud, draw it, write it, and/or talk to someone about it.

5. *Learn to contain the feeling.* This is a huge part of self-mastery. Hold your thoughts and don't express your feeling until you are in a safe place where you have time to process what you are feeling, either on your own or with someone you trust. Containing is not "stuffing" the feeling; it's giving yourself a choice of when and how you will express yourself.

You drew your container on pages 26 and 79. It is important to practice "using" your container so that it becomes easy to do. Then you can use it in your mind for containing your feelings when you need to.

On the body below, write the names of your feelings in the places where you experience them. You can use colors, words, phrases, and/or pictures to describe where you experience each feeling.

EXPRESSING FEELINGS

1. Think of the unspoken rules about expressing feelings in your home when you were growing up. Place the feelings and experiences you learned to keep hidden "inside" the chest. You may use pictures or symbols instead of words, if you want.

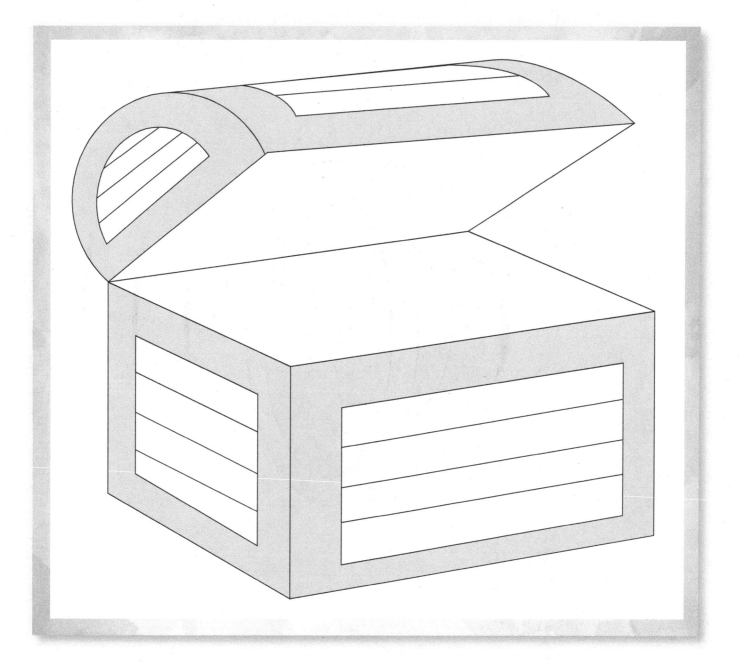

2. Describe the feelings and experiences you learned that you were free to share by showing them coming out of the speaker. You can use pictures or symbols instead of words.

The good news is that no matter what we learned in our families, we are learning new things in our group. Now we have the ability to try out and practice what we are learning.

REFLECTION

Reflect on what was meaningful to you in this session and what you want to remember. Then write or draw about it here.

BETWEEN-SESSIONS ACTIVITY

People choose to use alcohol, tobacco, and other drugs for all kinds of reasons. People may use as a way to change how they feel, to experiment, to feel older, to fit in, to feel more confident or sexy, to cope with intense or difficult feelings, or to get high or drunk. They may assume that if everyone else in their group is doing it, it's okay.

Although alcohol and other drugs may seem to "work" in the short term by giving a person a high or an escape from difficult feelings, substance use often causes more problems, such as an increased risk for abuse and addiction, physical health issues, mental health issues, and involvement in crime. In the long run, it creates more stress and difficulty in one's life.

Make a list of the costs and benefits (the − and the +) of choosing to use alcohol, tobacco, or other drugs.

Dealing with Life as It Happens

THIS SESSION

Anyone who uses alcohol, tobacco, or other drugs (including misusing prescription drugs) has the potential to become addicted. Addiction occurs among people of all ages, races, cultures, educational levels, income levels, and life experiences. However, some people are at greater risk of becoming addicted to alcohol or other drugs than other people. Research suggests that three types of factors affect a person's level of risk: biological, psychological, and environmental. In this session, you learn about the factors that affect a person's risk for addiction.

Stress occurs when experiences or circumstances feel overwhelming, overstimulating, or upsetting. The stress response can happen in negative and positive situations, and the response can be emotional and/or physical. This session helps you to explore different healthy strategies for coping with stress.

Spirituality can be difficult to describe. It is not the same as religion, and different people achieve it in different ways. Whatever form they take, spiritual practices help us to make sense of the world and can act as great sources of strength and guidance in our lives. This session helps you to understand different ways in which you can connect to something bigger and deeper that yourself.

This session also provides you with an easy way to remember the basics of self-care, including healthy connections with others, exercise, learning, healthy eating, and adequate sleep.

UNDERSTANDING ADDICTION

There are biological, psychological, and environmental factors that affect which people are more likely to become addicted.

Biological Factors

A tendency to become addicted may be genetic. This means that, if you have a family member who is addicted to alcohol or other drugs, you are at greater risk of becoming addicted. For example, immediate family members of alcoholics have a 60% greater risk of developing alcoholism.

Psychological Factors

Misuse of alcohol and other drugs can be linked to personality traits, such as risk taking, thrill seeking, aggressiveness, trouble controlling one's impulses, and coping with emotional pain.

Environmental Factors

Things around you may increase your risk of addiction. For example, use of alcohol or other drugs by parents or peers, stress in the family, stress at school or work, and the availability of drugs in your school and community may increase your risk.

The Power of Choice

Having a family history of substance misuse or certain psychological or social traits does not automatically mean that you will become addicted to alcohol, tobacco, or other drugs. At the same time, the absence of these factors is no guarantee that you will not. What can make the difference are the choices you make about your use of alcohol or other drugs (including the misuse of prescriptions).

1. Do you have family members who are addicted to alcohol or other drugs?
   ___yes ___no

2. What traits do you possess that you think might increase your risk of becoming addicted?

_____

_____

_____

_____

_____

_____

_____

_____

_____

3. What factors around you might increase your risk of becoming addicted?

_____

_____

_____

_____

_____

_____

_____

_____

COPING WITH STRESS

Stress is a response to something that happens that feels overwhelming, over-stimulating, or upsetting. Some people use alcohol, tobacco, and other drugs as a way to cope with stress. They try to use substances to numb their feelings, to relax, or to enjoy socializing. Although alcohol or other drugs may seem to work in the short term, they can end up causing more stress.

1. Overall, how would you rate your day-to-day stress?

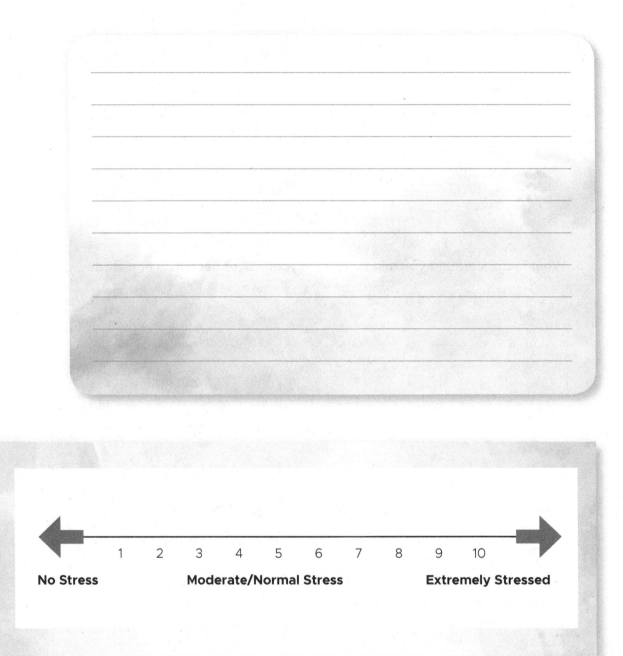

2. Describe a situation in which you felt a lot of stress:

- Where did you feel the stress in your body?

- How did it affect your ability to feel comfortable with yourself?

- How do you typically cope with stress?

- Is there any stress in your life that never goes away? If so, what is it?

_____

_____

_____

_____

_____

_____

_____

_____

_____

_____

Healthy Ways to Cope with Stress

- Eat a healthy diet.
- Take a break from electronics and social media.
- Get regular exercise.
- Ask for help when you need it.
- Balance life between school or work and fun.
- Use self-mastery techniques.
- Schedule your time in a realistic way; learn to manage your time.
- Accept things you can't change or control.
- Pay attention to your body's warning signs (headaches, stomachaches, feeling tired).
- Listen to music.
- Talk with a friend or a person you trust.
- Work on problems or challenges that are bothering you.
- Avoid keeping secrets.
- Don't isolate yourself.

Grounding and centering techniques (self-mastery techniques) are good ways to deal with stress. Grounding techniques can help us to realize that what we experienced in the past is not happening now. They also work when we are dealing with something in the present. Remember that there are additional techniques starting on page 168 in Appendix 2. that you can use.

You may want to add some new strategies here.

SPIRITUALITY

Spirituality is not the same as religion. A person can be religious without being spiritual and vice versa. A person also can be religious and spiritual.

Spirituality can be an experience of feeling a connection with something beyond oneself, connection with the earth and nature, or a sense of "wholeness" achieved by connection with others. People choose to practice spirituality in many ways, including, but not limited to quiet time; prayer; meditation; centering; activities such as singing and music; being out in nature; keeping a journal; attending a church, synagogue, mosque, or temple; and helping others in need. Just taking time to be in connection with yourself and the universe, whatever that may mean, is practicing spirituality. Whatever form they take, spiritual practices help us to make sense of the world and can act as great sources of strength and guidance.

• What does spirituality mean to you?

• What do you do to connect with your spirituality?

- What people, places, or things give you feelings of serenity and safety or a sense of purpose in your life?

SELF-CARE (SEEDS)

Here are the SEEDS for self-care of the brain:

    S—social connectivity: being in connection and relationship with others
    E—exercise: thirty minutes a day can make a big difference
    E—education: learn something new each day
    D—diet: the food we eat either nourishes or starves our brains
    S—sleep: our brains and our bodies need to rest and regenerate each day

REFLECTION

Reflect on what was meaningful to you in this session and what you want to remember. Then write or draw about it here.

BETWEEN-SESSIONS ACTIVITY

People choose to practice spirituality in many ways. Between now and the next session, interview two people and write about their answers to these questions:

1. How do they practice spirituality?

_____

_____

_____

_____

_____

_____

_____

_____

2. How does spirituality help them in their lives?

_____

_____

_____

_____

_____

_____

_____

_____

You may use the space below to finish writing or drawing the answers.

Endings and Beginnings

THIS SESSION

This is a time when you can begin to envision what you want your future to look like. To make this vision a reality, you will have to make important decisions. These decisions may be about things such as school, jobs, substance use, eating habits, sex, using power and control, staying in unhealthy relationships, finding healthy relationships, finances, and family matters. This session gives you tips for making decisions. It can help you learn to ask for help when you need it and it can help you to appreciate having a healthy support group.

At this end of our program, this session gives you an opportunity to express your appreciation for the other members of your group and to hear what they appreciate about you.

We extend all our best wishes for you for a healthy, happy, and successful future.

HEALING MASKS

1. On page 161, you will find the Front or Outside of a mask. The Back or Inside of the mask is on page 162.

2. Draw a line vertically down the middle of each of your masks, both the Front or Outside one and the Back or Inside one.

3. Then, on the left side of the Front or Outside mask, draw or write the past behaviors you have used that have caused harm to yourself or others or behaviors you've done to escape the pain of your past, such as using alcohol or other drugs.

4. On the right side of the Front or Outside mask, draw or write the positive and effective behaviors you'd like to replace them with.

5. On the left side of your Back or Inside mask, draw or write some of the negative thoughts, beliefs, emotions, and experiences of your past.

6. On the right side of the Back or Inside mask, draw or write the thoughts, emotions, and beliefs you'd like to experience in the future as you free yourself from the past.

The next page contains samples of some masks created by other participants. Please make your own mask all about you.

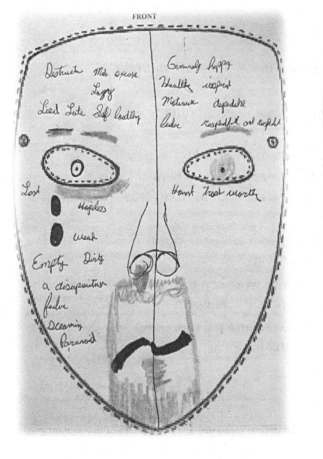
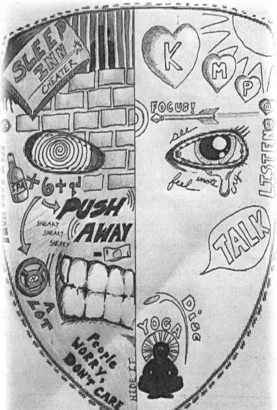
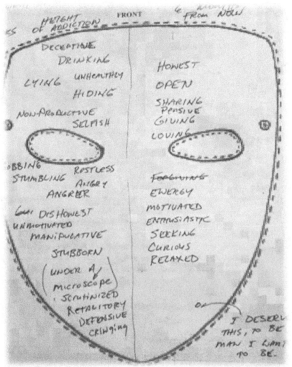

Healing Mask Samples

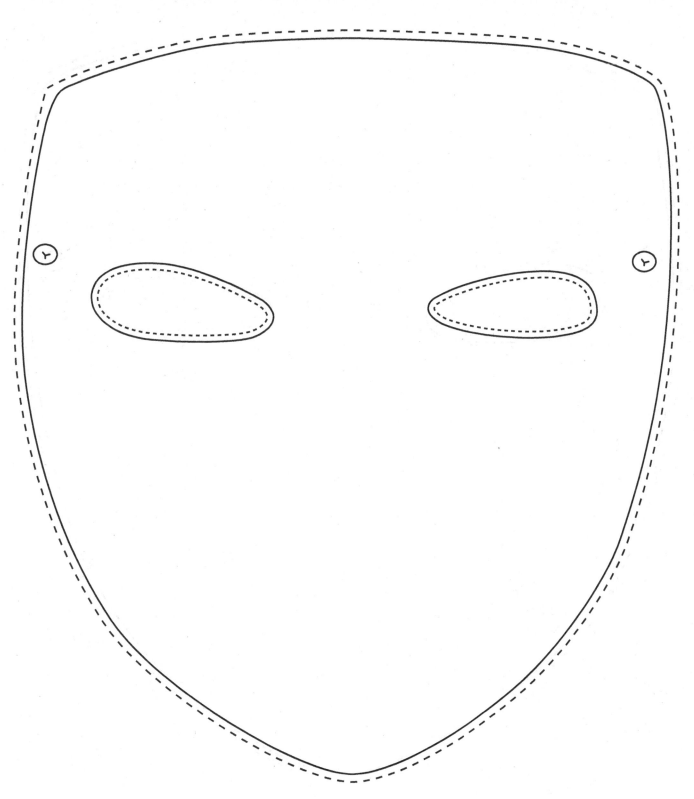

Healing Mask: Front or Outside

Source: Reprinted from S. S. Covington & R. Rodriguez. (2016). *Exploring Trauma: A Brief Intervention for Men* (p. 177). Center City, MN: Hazelden Publishing.

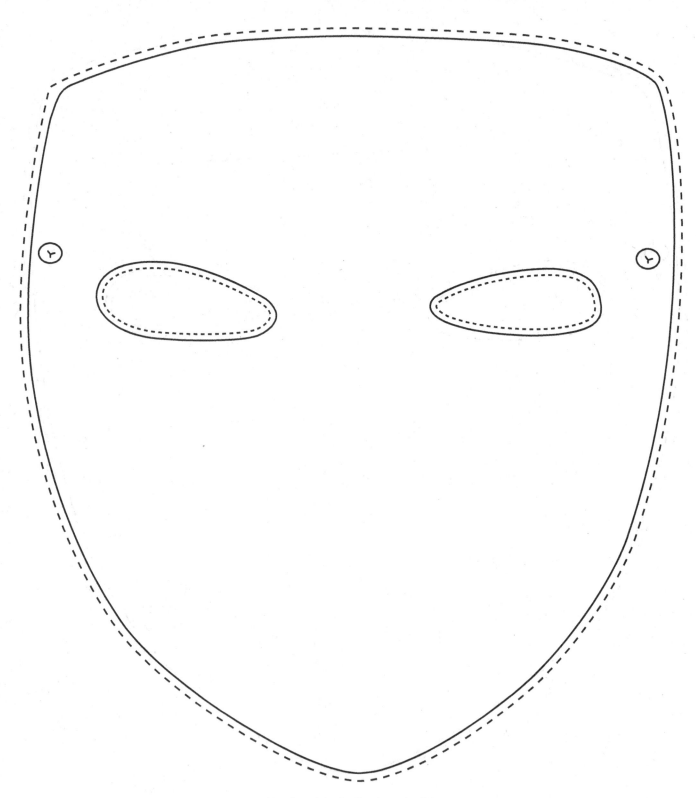

Healing Mask: Back or Inside

Source: Reprinted from S. S. Covington & R. Rodriguez. (2016). *Exploring Trauma: A Brief Intervention for Men* (p. 177). Center City, MN: Hazelden Publishing.

DECISION MAKING

You may have guessed that, in order to make your vision come true for yourself, you will have to make some difficult decisions about what to do and what not to do. These often are referred to as "crossroads" decisions. They are important parts of life and can affect the rest of your life.

Here are some examples:

- To use or not use alcohol, tobacco, and other drugs, including others' prescriptions
- To be sexually active with a partner or not
- To practice safe sex or not
- To stay in a relationship or to end it
- To join a club or organization or not
- To finish high school or to drop out
- To attend college or learn a trade or not
- To hang out with certain people or groups or not
- To seek help for traumatic experiences or not
- To stay in gang activity or not
- To engage in illegal activities or not

You may want to add some typical decisions from your group's list here.

_____

_____

_____

_____

_____

_____

_____

Decision-Making Tips

1. Don't try to be perfect; mistakes and failures are our greatest teachers.

2. Pay attention to the details; it's the little things that help us do big things.

3. Remind yourself that you are in charge of the person you will be ten years from now, that your decisions now will shape your future.

4. Do a cost-benefit check.

5. Find someone who has gone through the same thing as you are experiencing and ask about how and what the person decided and how it worked out for that person.

6. Get a second opinion. Talk to more than one person. Try to include someone who has a different point of view from the first person you asked.

7. Make a plan and stick to it.

CELEBRATING ONE ANOTHER

Appendices

Local Resources (Session Six)

If you or someone you know is being abused, here are some resources that can be helpful:

National

1. The National Domestic Violence Hotline: 800-799-SAFE (7233)
2. MenHealing.org
3. Men's Resource Center: 616-456-1178
4. National Sexual Assault Hotline: 800-656-HOPE

Local Resources for Boys/Young Men in Abusive Relationship

Name of Program	Type of Service	Address and Phone

Local Resources for Boys/Young Men Who Have Experienced Abuse

Name of Program	Type of Service	Address and Phone

Resources for Boys/Young Men Who Want to Stop Hurting Others

Name of Program	Type of Service	Address and Phone

Local Resources for LGBTQI Youth

Name of Program	Type of Service	Address and Phone

APPENDIX 2

Self-Mastery Techniques: Grounding and Self-Soothing

The Five Senses (Session One)

1. Close your eyes or, if you're not comfortable doing that, look at a fixed spot on the floor in front of you.
2. Relax for a few moments. Take a few deep breaths and exhale slowly.
3. Open your eyes when you are ready.
4. Silently, identify five things you can see around you.
5. Now identify four things you can feel or touch.
6. Identify three things you can hear.
7. Now identify two things you can smell.
8. Finally, identify what you can taste.
9. Now open your eyes and come back to the here and now.

My Place (Session Two)

1. Sit comfortably with good posture, with your back straight, and place your feet flat on the floor.
2. Place your hands either palms up or palms down on your lap and relax.
3. Close your eyes or look at a fixed spot on the floor in front of you.
4. Relax your shoulders and slowly roll your neck in a circle from left to right.
5. Now roll your neck in a circle from right to left.
6. Holding your head still, allow yourself to notice how you're breathing.
7. Then inhale gently through your nose and exhale fully through your mouth.
8. Feel the temperature of the air as it comes in through your nose.
9. Feel the air as it leaves your body when you breathe out through your mouth.

10. Don't force your breath; let it flow naturally and slowly.

11. If you begin to think about different things that are happening in your life outside the room you're in, just notice them without judgment and let them drift past like clouds in the sky as you return to noticing your breath.

12. Continue to be aware of your breath as it slowly flows in and out.

13. Choose an image of a place that means calmness or safety to you. It can be a real place or you can use your imagination.

14. Take a moment to breathe in all the beauty of this place.

15. Then breathe out any negative or distracting thoughts you may have.

16. Repeat breathing in your calm or safe place and breathing out any negative thoughts.

17. Do this a few more times.

18. When you're ready, return to the here and now.

My Place (Variation) (Session Two)

1. Sit quietly and let yourself relax.

2. Close your eyes or look at a fixed spot on the floor in front of you.

3. Put one hand on your chest and one hand on your stomach.

4. Take a couple of normal breaths. You probably will find that you are feeling these breaths mostly in your chest.

5. Try moving your breath deeper into your lower abdomen so that your hand on your stomach moves as you breathe.

6. Close your mouth and press your tongue lightly to the roof of your mouth. Let your jaw relax.

7. Take a breath slowly in through your nose as you silently count to four.

8. Slowly exhale and feel the breath leaving your nose as you silently count to four one more time.

9. Try it again.

10. As thoughts come up, acknowledge them and then return your focus to your breathing.

11. Keep breathing deeply. Let your belly fill with air each time.

12. Breathe in through your nose and count to four.

13. Breath out slowly, counting to four.

14. Now, picture a place in your mind that means peace or calm to you. It can be a place you've been to before or one you imagine.

15. Only you are there, no one else.

16. As you continue to breathe, take in the beauty of this place,
    - the temperature,
    - the sounds,
    - and the way you feel when you are here.

17. This is your place, where you can be safe, where nothing can harm you.

18. You can come here anytime simply by closing your eyes and breathing as you've practiced.

19. Now, slowly become more aware of your surroundings and, when you are ready, open your eyes.

Palms Up, Palms Down (Session Three)

1. Sit up straight in your seat, with both feet on the floor.

2. Close your eyes or, if you're not comfortable closing your eyes, look at a spot on the floor in front of you.

3. Breathe naturally and slowly.

4. Now begin to breathe deeper into your belly.

5. Breathe in to a count of four.

6. Breathe out to a count of six.

7. Repeat that a couple of times.

8. Now, hold both your arms outstretched, with the palms of your hands turned up and touching side by side, as though someone was about to put something in your hands.

9. Visualize a list of all the thoughts and feelings that are bothering you right now.

10. Imagine placing all your cares, concerns, problems, and troubling memories into your hands.

11. All these negative emotions and thoughts are out of your bodies and lying in your hands.

12. Imagine the weight of holding all these problems, these negative thoughts and emotions, in your hands. Feel the strain of carrying them.

13. Now, slowly and carefully turn your hands upside down, so that your palms face the floor. Let all the problems, stresses, bad feelings, and negativity fall to the floor. For now, drop everything that might distract you from our group.

14. When you are ready, open your eyes.

The Container (Sessions Three, Six, and Seven)

1. Sit comfortably with good posture, with your feet on the ground and your hands in a comfortable position on your lap.
2. Close your eyes or look at a spot on the floor in front of you.
3. Tune in to your breathing. Slowly and smoothly breathe in.
4. Feel the temperature of the air as it passes into your lungs.
5. Exhale slowly and smoothly.
6. Continue breathing in and out smoothly.
7. Now imagine a container. It can be any object, any shape you want. It only has to have a lid to hold things securely inside.
8. As you continue to breathe deeply and smoothly, become aware of any powerful emotions you may feel right now. These may include feelings of hurt or shame or frustration or whatever.
9. Slowly, one by one, place all these feelings inside your container.
10. Once you've placed all of them in the container, tightly close the lid.
11. These feelings or emotions have not gone away. You're merely putting them inside the container for now so that you can interact with the world around you in the present. You can deal with these feelings and emotions later when it is a better time to do so.
12. When you've closed your container and are ready, return to the here and now.

Breathing (Session Four)

1. Sit comfortably, with your back straight and your feet flat on the ground.
2. Close your eyes or look at a spot on the floor in front of you.
3. Become aware of your body. Scan your body for any sensations or tension you may feel.
4. Then go inside your body and focus on your heartbeat and your body temperature.
5. Begin to breathe deeply but smoothly. It may help if you count to four when you breathe in.
6. Now exhale to the count of six.
7. Repeat this a couple of times while being aware of your heartbeat and of your body temperature. As you continue to breathe deeply and smoothly, you may feel your heartbeat slow down and your temperature feel warm and comfortable.
8. As you continue to breathe deeply and slowly, you may feel that the sensation or tension you felt before may be beginning to ease and that you feel calmer.

9. Continue to breathe while relaxing all your facial muscles: your forehead, your cheeks, and your jaw.

10. Continue to breathe and enjoy this moment of self-mastery.

11. Now open your eyes and return to the here and now.

Healing Light (Session Five)

1. Sit up straight in your seat, with both feet on the floor.

2. Close your eyes or, if you're not comfortable closing your eyes, look at a spot on the floor in front of you.

3. Breathe naturally and slowly.

4. Now begin to breathe deeper into your belly.

5. Breathe in to the count of four.

6. Breathe out to the count of six.

7. Repeat that a couple of times.

8. Now, as you continue to breath, scan your body for any place where you might feel tightness or soreness.

9. Focus on that spot and give the sensation a color. It could be black or dark red or any other color you want.

10. Continue to breathe and now imagine that you can feel a light above you. Give it a color.

11. Allow this healing light to come in through the top of your head and into your shoulders. Let this light travel to where you felt the tightness or soreness before.

12. Continue to breathe deeply and imagine the color of the healing light mixing with the color or your tightness or soreness and then begin to dissolve it.

13. Feel the tension and soreness continue to ease as you breathe for a few more breaths.

14. When you are ready, open your eyes.

Progressive Muscle Relaxation (Session Five)

1. Get comfortable in your seat or lying down.

2. Close your eyes or look at a spot on the floor in front of you.

3. Take a few moments to relax, breathing in and out in slow, deep breaths.

4. Now focus your attention on your feet. Take a moment to focus on the way your feet feel.

5. Slowly tense the muscles in your feet, squeezing them as tightly as you can. Hold this for a count of ten.

6. Relax your feet. Focus on the tension flowing away and the way your feet feel relaxed.

7. Stay in this relaxed state for a moment, breathing slowly and deeply.

8. Now tense the muscles in your calves. Hold this for a count of ten.

9. Relax your calves. Feel the tension flowing away. Breathe slowly and deeply.

10. Now tense the muscles in your thighs. Hold them tight for a count of ten.

11. Relax the muscles in your thighs. Feel the tension flow away. Breathe slowly and deeply.

12. Tense the muscles in your hips and buttocks. Hold this for a count of ten.

13. Now relax your hips and buttocks. Feel the tension flowing out. Keep breathing.

14. Tense the muscles in your abdomen. Hold them tight for a count of ten.

15. Relax your abdomen. Feel the tension flowing out. Breathe.

16. Now tense up your chest muscles. Hold this for a count of ten.

17. Relax your chest muscles. Let the tension flow out. Breathe.

18. Tense up your back muscles. Hold this while you count to ten.

19. Relax your back. Feel the tension oozing out. Breathe.

20. Now tense the muscles in your arms and hands. Hold them tight for a count of ten.

21. Relax your arms and hands. Let the tension flow out. Breathe.

22. Tense the muscles in your neck and shoulders. Hold them tight while you count to ten.

23. Relax your neck and shoulders. Let the tension flow out of them while you breathe slowly and deeply.

24. Tense the muscles in your face. Hold for a count of ten.

25. Relax your facial muscles. Breathe slowly and deeply.

26. Now open your eyes.

Square Breathing (Sessions Six and Eight)

1. Sit comfortably in your chair without slouching.

2. Close your eyes or look at a spot on the floor in front of you.

3. Breathe in. One, two, three, four.

4. Hold the breath. One, two, three, four.

5. Exhale. One, two, three, four.

6. Hold the exhale. One, two, three, four.

7. Repeat. Breathe in. One, two, three, four.

8. Hold the breath. One, two, three, four.

9. Exhale. One, two, three, four.

10. Hold the exhale. One, two, three, four.

11. Repeat while thinking to yourselves that you are in a safe space.

12. Breathe in. One, two, three, four.

13. Hold the breath. One, two, three, four.

14. Exhale. One, two, three, four.

15. Hold the exhale. One, two, three, four.

16. Repeat one last time, while you give yourself permission to be open-minded.

17. Breathe in. One, two, three, four.

18. Hold the breath. One, two, three, four.

19. Exhale. One, two, three, four.

20. Hold the exhale. One, two, three, four.

21. Relax for a moment.

Soothing Activities (Session Six)

- Taking long, deep breaths
- Listening to music
- Taking a long, hot shower or bath
- Taking a walk
- Thinking about a good memory
- Remembering a safe place that you find very soothing (perhaps the beach or mountains or a favorite room) and focusing on everything about it: the sounds, colors, shapes, objects, textures, and smells
- Thinking about people you care about and looking at photographs of them or imagine them smiling at you
- Thinking of your favorite animal, season, car, food, time of day, or television show
- Talking to a trusted friend
- Writing in a journal
- Reading
- Painting or drawing
- Writing down what you want to say to someone

- Saying kind statements to yourself, such as "You are a good person going through a hard time; you'll get through this"
- Say a coping statement, such as "I can handle this" or "This feeling will pass"
- Reciting the words to an inspiring song, quotation, or poem that makes you feel better
- Planning a safe treat for yourself, such as a piece of candy or a favorite food or a nice dinner
- Thinking of something you are looking forward to in the next week, such as spending time with a person you like

Mental Grounding (Session Six)

- Describe your environment in detail using all your senses. For example, "The walls are white, there are five brown chairs, there is a wooden bookshelf against the wall . . . ." Describe objects, sounds, textures, colors, smells, shapes, numbers, and temperature. You can do this anywhere.
- Play a "categories" game with yourself. Try to think of "types of dogs," "musicians," "states that begin with 'A,'" "cars," "funny television shows," "writers," "sports stars," "songs," or "state capitals."
- Do an age progression. Sometimes when we are emotionally triggered, we may feel like we're younger, maybe even a little kid. If you are feeling younger than you actually are, then you may have regressed to a younger age. You can slowly work your way back up by saying "I'm now nine," "I'm now ten," "I'm now eleven," and so on until you are back to your current age.
- Describe an everyday activity in great detail. For example, describe a meal that you can cook by going through all the steps. Or shooting a basketball or passing a football.
- Use an image: Glide along on skates away from your pain, change the television channel to get to a better show, or think of a wall as a buffer between you and your pain.
- Say a safety statement, such as "My name is _____; I am safe right now. I am in the present, not the past. I am located in _____; the date is _____."
- Read something, saying each word to yourself. Or read each letter backwards so that you focus on the letters and not the meanings of the words.
- Use humor. Think of something funny to jolt yourself out of your mood.

- Count to ten or say the alphabet very slowly.
- Repeat a favorite saying or poem to yourself over and over.

Physical Grounding (Session Six)

- Run cool or warm water over your hands.
- Grab tightly onto your chair as hard as you can.
- Touch various objects around you, such as a pen, keys, your clothing, the table, the walls. Notice textures, colors, materials, weight, and temperature. Compare objects you touch: Is one colder? Lighter?
- Dig your heels into the floor, literally "grounding" them. Notice the tension centered in your heels as you do this. Remind yourself that you are connected to the ground.
- Carry a grounding object in your pocket, such as a small rock, ring, piece of cloth, or something else that you can touch whenever you feel anxious or stressed.
- Jump up and down.
- Notice your body: the weight of your body in the chair, the feel of your back against the chair. Wiggle your toes. You are connected to the world.
- Stretch. Extend your fingers, arms, or legs as far as you can; roll your head around.
- Walk slowly, noticing each footstep, saying "left," and "right" with each step.
- Eat something and describe the flavors in detail to yourself.
- Focus on your breathing, noticing each inhale and exhale. Repeat a pleasant word to yourself on each inhale (for example, a favorite color or a soothing word such as "safe" or "easy").

Noticing (Session Six)

1. Sit comfortably in your chair without slouching, with your feet on the floor.
2. Notice how that feels. Notice your bottom sitting in the chair.
3. Notice the temperature of the room and how that feels.
4. Choose an object in the room and look at it.
5. Think of what it might feel like.
6. Pretend that you are examining it.
7. As you look, breathe slowly in and out.
8. Now bring your attention back to the here and now.

Breathing (Variation) (Session Seven)

1. Sit comfortably in your chair without slouching, with your feet on the floor.
2. Breathe in and silently count to four. One, two, three, four.
3. Hold it. One, two, three, four.
4. Breathe out while counting to four. One, two, three, four.
5. Hold again. One, two, three, four.
6. Repeat this four more times.

ADDITIONAL GROUNDING/SELF-MASTERY ACTIVITIES
Taking an Emotional Time Out

1. Sit comfortably in a chair and close your eyes or look at the floor in front of you.
2. Inhale through your nose and hold it for a few seconds.
3. Exhale through your mouth and hold it for a few seconds.
4. Continue to do this slowly for seven more complete breaths.
5. Now visualize how you'd like your physical body to feel.
6. Imagine the kind of energy and well-being you want for yourself. Visualize how that feels. Try to experience what this would feel like for you.
7. Say an affirmation to yourself three times. Say something that inspires you. Some people say things like, "I am whole," "I am healing myself," and "I am a worthwhile human being." Pick an affirmation that means something to you.

Physical Grounding
Activity 1

1. Stand up.
2. Feel your feet on the ground. Notice the springiness in your legs. Feel the way your feet connect with the ground, almost like a magnet is holding you there or as if you're a tree with big, strong roots.
3. With your feet firmly planted, sway slowly from side to side from the ankles and then sway forward and backward. This will help you find your center of gravity. It usually is located in your lower belly area.
4. As you continue to sway, place your hands on your lower belly and sense your center of gravity.
5. Now sit back down in your chair. Relax.
6. Be sure that your feet are firmly on the ground. Place your hands on your lower belly again and feel the energy coming into that area through your feet.

1. Sit with your feet on the floor and notice how that feels.
2. Notice your bottom sitting in the chair.
3. Notice the temperature of the room and how that feels.
4. Choose an object in the room and look at it.
5. Think of what it feels like.
6. As you look, breathe slowly in and out.

Activity 3

1. Lie on your back.
2. Put one hand on your chest and one hand on your belly. Take a couple of normal breaths.
3. You'll probably find that you're feeling these breaths mostly in your chest.
4. Try moving your breath deeper into your lower belly, so your hand on your belly moves up and down as you breathe.
5. Try it again.
6. You'll find that you're breathing more slowly and more completely than usual.
7. Keep breathing deeply, but blow the air out of your mouth, rather than out of your nose.
8. Let your belly fill with air each time.
9. Repeat this at least six times.

Activity 4

1. Sit in a comfortable position with your feet on the floor.
2. Concentrate on your breathing: breathing in, pausing, and breathing out.
3. Feel your body as it expands from the center and releases back toward the center.
4. With each breath, breathe a little deeper, moving the air deeper down into your abdomen.
5. As you breathe in, take in "good things," such as good thoughts about yourself, hope, courage, safety, and joy.
6. As you breathe out, let go of things you don't want in your life, such as self-criticism, violence, hatred, anger, and fear.
7. Do this for two or three minutes.

1. Find a place where you can walk without shoes and socks. It may be a park, the beach, a garden, the grass in your yard, a room in your home, or a room where you are now. Start with bare feet.

2. Walk as slowly as you can. Focus on the movement of each part of your body: your foot, your leg, and so on.

3. As you walk, breathe deeply and think about your feet as they connect with the ground.

4. Slow down even more. Move just as slowly as you can.

5. Be aware of every tiny movement.

6. Look around and take in your surroundings.

7. Be in the present and feel the connection with your world.

Mental Grounding
Activity 6

1. Relax. Take a deep breath.

2. Look at the room around you. Focus on the size of the room.

3. Focus on the color and texture of the walls.

4. Notice the height of the ceiling.

5. Notice the lights.

6. Notice the windows, if there are any.

7. Look at the doors.

8. Look at the furniture.

9. Pay attention to any pictures or other objects in the room.

10. Think of today's date and what time it is.

11. Think of what city you're in.

12. Now focus on yourself. Think of your name.

13. Think of your age.

14. Think of the grounding activities you have done recently.

Relaxation
Activity 7

1. Lie on your back on the floor. If you would rather sit, that is fine.

2. Close your eyes or lower your eyelids.

3. Take a deep breath in while you silently count to four.

4. Now breathe out slowly to a count of four. Try to breathe from your belly, not just from your chest.

5. Breathe in again.

6. And out again.

7. Repeat the slow breathing two more times.

8. In your mind, picture your favorite safe place to be. Imagine yourself being there.

9. Keep breathing deeply and very slowly.

10. Starting with your head and moving down your body, let the muscles in your face relax. Let your forehead relax. Let your cheekbones relax. Let your jaw joints relax.

11. Let your neck and upper shoulders relax. As you exhale, imagine all the tension going out with each breath. Let it go.

12. Let your hands and arms go limp next to you.

13. Let your chest, stomach, and the whole middle part of your body relax.

14. Keep breathing in and out.

15. Let your hips and your buttocks relax.

16. Let your upper legs and lower legs relax.

17. Let your feet and toes relax.

18. Let your whole body relax. Breathe in and out.

19. Keep imagining the safe place you picked. Enjoy where you are; enjoy the tension going out of your body. Be relaxed, almost floating and weightless, as you stay in that image.

20. Now open your eyes.

APPENDIX
3

Yoga Poses
(Session Six)

BREATH OF JOY
Purpose

The Breath of Joy exercise connects the use of breath with body movements to aid a physical and emotional release of tension. The person then feels relaxed yet energized. This exercise is beneficial for letting go (or at least loosening the grip) of long-held anger or grief that has been stored in the physical body or in habitual thought patterns that no longer are supportive for growth. This physical and emotional release assists people to become willing to adopt new ideas, thought patterns, and behaviors for personal development.

Practice

The Breath of Joy consists of three quick and consecutive inhalations through the nose and one audible exhalation through the mouth. These breaths are synchronized with arm movements to engage the whole body.

Begin in a standing position with the feet about hip-width apart. Take a short inhalation through the nose while bringing the arms straight out in front of the chest. Take another quick inhalation through the nose while opening the arms

wide in a T shape. Take one last inhalation while reaching the arms straight over-head. With an audible "ahh" sound, exhale through the mouth while bringing the arms in a sweeping motion down to the side of the body. For those who have limited mobility, a modification is to come down only halfway on the exhale.

Once the pattern of synchronizing the breath with movement is comfortable, create a fuller body expression by bending the knees while dropping the chest into a forward bend during the exhalation and letting the arms swing down and past the hips.

SEATED PIGEON
Purpose

The Seated Pigeon pose provides a deep stretch through the side of the hip and the band of tissues that connects the outer hip and the outer side of the knee. This band of tissues often is tight, which can cause lower-back pain, knee challenges, and aggravation of the sciatic nerve—sometimes felt as "shooting" pain through the outer hip, leg, or groin. Giving these tissues a modest stretch with this pose can bring relief from aches and also increase physical comfort when sitting or walking.

Practicing this pose also can provide an emotional release of stress or trauma around the hips. It can aid in the release of anger or depression. Some people experience a physical feeling of release or relief, and others exhibit an emotional response, such as tears.

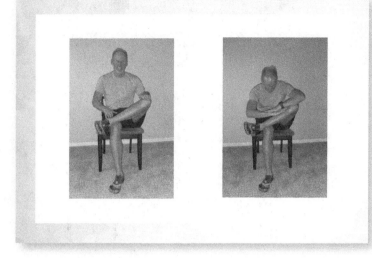

Practice

Begin while seated in a chair with both feet on the ground. Place the left foot on the right knee, so that the legs resemble a number 4 when looking down at the shape. Some people feel a tug immediately on the side of the left hip or buttock. It may radiate down the side of the leg toward the knee. If it isn't felt in these areas, simply lean forward. As the torso moves forward toward the legs, the tension to the outer hip is increased. You can hold on to the seat of the chair for support or lean your forearms on your knees.

Hold the pose for one to three minutes for optimal results. Then repeat with the leg positions reversed.

MODIFIED TRIANGLE
Purpose

The Modified Triangle exercise targets tissues in the inner legs, lower back, and hips. It offers a nice stretch to the side of the body and ribs. The spinal twist massages and supports the spinal column and soothes the nerves that branch out from each of the vertebrae and connect with every other part of the body. Symbolically, the triangle, or pyramid shape, represents the balance and unity between the three interconnected aspects of being: mind, body, and spirit.

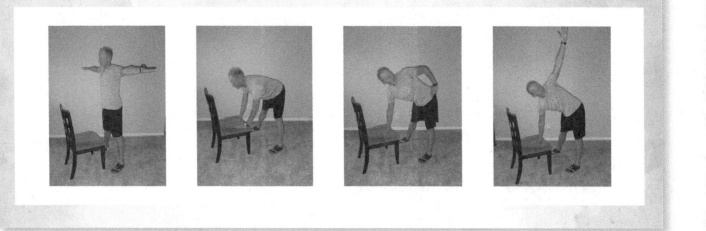

Practice

Stand in front of the seat of a chair. Hold the arms out to the sides in a T position and then open the legs wide until the ankles align under the wrists. The wide stance offers a solid and steady foundation to the pose. Place both hands on the seat of the chair (about the width of the shoulders), keeping the arms straight. Bend forward from the hips. This may yield a nice hamstring stretch and can be held for several breaths.

To continue into the Modified Triangle pose, with the legs straight, keep the left foot facing forward but pivot the right foot out so that its toes point to the side. This will create a tug to the inner right leg. Next, reach toward the ceiling or sky with the left arm and hand. The left hip will follow so that your chest and gaze will be toward the left. Hold the pose for five to ten breaths. This exercise stretches the inner leg while rotating the spine in a gentle twist, stimulating the tissues of the lower back.

If you have difficulty reaching upward with a straight arm, you can place your reaching hand on your hip instead and enjoy the twist of the spine.

Bring both hands back to the seat and repeat the exercise on the other side (the right foot points forward as the left foot pivots to the side and the right hand reaches upward).

TWISTED BRANCHES TO OPEN WINGS
Purpose

The Twisted Branches and Open Wings poses complement one another and offer muscular release to the upper back, shoulders, and chest. When practiced together, they work in harmony to stimulate the lungs and heart. Lungs symbolically represent the ability to let go of stagnant energy (exhaling) and invite in new life and possibility (inhaling). Combining breath and movement aids the transformation of grief into a desire to explore the fullness of life and to feel safe doing so. Stimulating the heart serves the transition out of anxiety and into the ability to trust one's intuition and insight, create healthy boundaries, and experience joy.

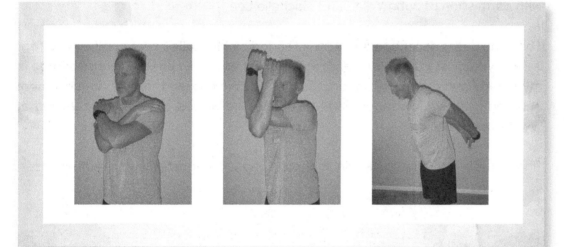

Practice

Because each person's bone structure is different, Twisted Branches can be performed in a number of ways so that you can find the one that feels best for your body. The gentlest pose is simply to cross the arms in front of the chest, resting the crossed hands on the shoulders in what looks like a self-hug. Do this while taking five to ten breaths.

The second option is to cross the upper arms by resting the elbow of one arm in the soft elbow crease of the opposite arm. The hands may be back to back or you may be able to bring the palms together. Crossing the arms in front causes the shoulder blades to stretch, which facilitates the release of tension in the upper back. Take five to ten breaths.

Then release the arms and clasp the hands together behind the back to create the Open Wings pose. Depending on your bone structure and level of comfort, the arms can be straight or the elbows can be bent. This pose compresses and relaxes the tissues of the upper back and the shoulder blades, while simultaneously offering a stretch across the chest.

Drop the chin toward the chest to provide a new level of release in the back of the head, neck, and upper back. Hold the pose while taking five to ten breaths.

Repeat Twisted Branches with the other arm on top and then complete another Open Wing pose.

The yoga instructions were provided by Machelle Lee and are adapted from *Beyond Violence*. Copyright 2013 by S. Covington. This material is reproduced with permission of John Wiley and Machelle Lee.

The yoga poses described are recommended by Machelle Lee, a certified and registered yoga instructor and massage therapist. Machelle has a master's degree in mythology and depth psychology. Since 1991, she has led therapeutic-movement and yoga classes in various parts of the United States. She can be reached at www.machellelee.com.

Photographs provided by Kevin Johnson, who is demonstrating the actual poses.

Redefining Gender (Session Ten)

Affirming pronouns: Refers to the most respectful and accurate pronouns for a person, as defined by that person. This is also sometimes referred to as "preferred gender pronouns," although this phrasing is increasingly outdated. To ascertain someone's affirming pronouns, ask: "What are your pronouns?"

Agender: Describes a person who does not identify as having a gender identity that can be categorized as man or woman or who identifies as not having a gender identity.

Androgynous: A combination of masculine and feminine traits or a nontraditional gender expression.

Bigender: A person who experiences gender identity as two genders at the same time or whose gender identity may vary between two genders. These may be masculine and feminine or could include nonbinary identities.

Cisgender (pronounced sis-gender): A term to describe a person whose gender identity matches the biological sex they were assigned at birth. (It is sometimes abbreviated as "cis.")

Deadnaming: Having people use the name a trans person was given at birth instead of their chosen name.

Gender binary: The idea that gender is strictly an either-or option of male/man/masculine or female/woman/feminine based on sex assigned at birth rather than a continuum or spectrum of gender identities and expressions. The gender binary is considered to be limiting and problematic for those who do not fit neatly into the either-or categories.

Gender conforming: A person whose gender expression is consistent with the cultural norms expected for that gender. According to these norms, boys and men should be masculine and girls and women should be feminine. Not all cisgender people are gender conforming and not all transgender people are gender nonconforming. (For example, a transgender woman may have a very feminine gender expression.)

Gender dysphoria: This is the medical diagnosis for being transgender, as defined by the American Psychiatric Association's *Diagnostic and Statistical Manual of Mental Disorders*, fifth edition (*DSM-5*). The inclusion of gender dysphoria is controversial in transgender communities because it implies that being transgender is a mental illness rather than a valid identity. But because a formal diagnosis is generally required in order to receive or provide treatment in the United States, it does enable access to medical care for some people who wouldn't ordinarily be eligible to receive it.

Gender expression: A person's outward gender presentation, usually including personal style, clothing, hairstyle, makeup, jewelry, vocal inflection, and body language. Gender expression is typically categorized as masculine, feminine, or androgynous. All people express a gender. Gender expression can be congruent with a person's gender identity or not.

Genderfluid: Someone whose gender identity or expression shifts between man/masculine and woman/feminine or falls somewhere along this spectrum.

Gender identity: A person's deep-seated, internal sense of who they are as a gendered being: the gender with which they identify themselves.

Gender marker: The designation (male, female, or another) that appears on a person's official records, such as a birth certificate or driver's license. The gender marker on a transgender person's documents is their sex assigned at birth unless they legally change it in parts of the world that allow it.

Gender nonconforming: A person whose gender expression is perceived as being inconsistent with cultural norms expected for that gender. Specifically, boys or men who are not "masculine enough" or are feminine, or girls or women who are not "feminine enough" or are masculine. Not all transgender people are gender nonconforming, and not all gender-nonconforming people identify as transgender. Cisgender people may also be gender nonconforming. Gender nonconformity is often inaccurately confused with sexual orientation.

Genderqueer: Someone whose gender identity is neither man nor woman, is between or beyond genders, or is some combination of genders.

Intersex: A category that describes a person with a disorder of sexual development (DSD), a reproductive, genetic, genital, or hormonal configuration that results in a body that often can't be easily cat-egorized as male or female. Intersex is frequently confused with transgender, but the two are completely distinct. A more familiar term, hermaphrodite, is considered outdated and offensive.

LGBTQI: An acronym used to refer to lesbian, gay, bisexual, transgender, queer or questioning, and intersex individuals and communities. LGBTQ is not a synonym for "nonheterosexual," because that incorrectly implies that transgender is a sexual orientation rather than a gender identity. Variants include LGBT and LGBQ.

Medical transition: A long-term series of medical interventions that utilize hormonal treatments and/or surgical interventions to change a person's body to be more congruent with their gender identity. Medical transition is the approved medical treatment for Gender Dysphoria.

Nonbinary: A spectrum of gender identities and expressions, often based on the rejection of the assumption that gender is strictly an either-or option of male/man/masculine or female/woman/feminine, based on the sex assigned at birth. Terms include "agender," "bi-gender," "gender-queer," "genderfluid," and "pangender."

Pronouns: Affirming pronouns are the most respectful and accurate pro-nouns for a person as defined by that person. It's best to ask which pro-nouns a person uses. In addition to the familiar "he," "she," and "they," newly created nongendered pronouns include "zie" and "per."

Puberty suppression: A medical process that pauses the hormonal changes that activate puberty in young adolescents. The result is a purposeful delay of the development of secondary sexual character-istics (such as breast growth, testicular enlargement, facial hair, body fat redistribution, and voice changes). Suppression allows more time to make decisions about hormonal interventions and can prevent the increased dysphoria that often accompanies puberty for transgender youth.

Queer: An umbrella term for a range of people who are not heterosexual and/or cisgender. It has been historically used as a slur; some have reclaimed it as affirming, but others still consider it derogatory.

Same-gender loving: A label sometimes used by members of the African-American/Black community to express an alternative sexual orientation without relying on terms and symbols of European descent. The term emerged in the early 1990s with the intention of offering Black women who love women and Black men who love men a voice—a way of identifying and being that resonated with the uniqueness of Black culture. (Sometimes abbreviated "SGL.")

Sex assigned at birth: The determination of a person's sex based on the visual appearance of the genitals at birth. The sex someone is labeled at birth.

Sexual orientation: A person's feelings of attraction toward other people. A person may be attracted to people of the same sex, of the opposite sex, of both sexes, or without reference to sex or gender. Some people do not experience sexual attraction and may identify as asexual. Sexual orientation is about attraction to other people (external), while gender identity is a deep-seated sense of self (internal).

Social transition: A transgender person's process of a creating a life that is congruent with their gender identity, which often includes asking others to use a name, pronouns, and gender that is more congruent with their gender identity. It also may involve a person changing their gender expression to match their gender identity.

Transgender: Sometimes abbreviated as "trans," this is an adjective used to describe people whose gender identities do not match the biological sex assigned at birth. It can refer to a range of identities, including transgender boys and men—those who identify as a boy or man but were assigned the female label at birth—and transgender girls and women—those who identify as a girl or woman but were assigned the male label at birth.

Transgender men and boys: People who identify as male but were assigned female at birth. Also sometimes referred to as trans men.

Transgender women and girls: People who identify as female but were assigned male at birth. Also sometimes referred to as trans women.

Transsexual: This is an older term used to refer to a transgender person who has had hormonal and/or surgical interventions to change his or her body to be more aligned with his or her gender identity. "Transgender" has generally become the term of choice.

Two spirit: A term used by Native and Indigenous Peoples to indicate that they embody both a masculine and a feminine spirit. Is sometimes also used to describe Native People of diverse sexual orientations and has nuanced meanings in various indigenous subcultures.

Source: An adaption of Eli R. Green and Luca Maurer. (2015). *The Teaching Transgender Toolkit: A Facilitator's Guide to Increasing Knowledge, Decreasing Prejudice & Building Skills*. Ithaca, NY: Planned Parenthood of the Southern Finger Lakes: Out for Health. www.teachingtransgender.org.

FEEDBACK FORM

Dear Participant:

I would appreciate hearing about your experience with *A Young Man's Guide to Self-Mastery*. Any information or feedback you would like to share with me will be greatly appreciated.

Describe yourself:

Where did you participate in this program?

Describe your overall experience with the program:

What did you find most useful?

Why? How?

What did you find least useful?

Why? How?

What was missing from this program that you wish had been covered?

Other comments or suggestions:

Thank you for your input.

Please return this form to:
Stephanie S. Covington, Ph.D.
Institute for Relational Development
Center for Gender and Justice
7946 Ivanhoe Avenue, Suite 201B
La Jolla, CA 92037
Fax: (858) 454-8598
E-mail: sc@stephaniecovington.com
www.stephaniecovington.com

ABOUT THE AUTHORS

Stephanie S. Covington, PhD, LCSW, is an internationally recognized clinician, organizational consultant, and lecturer. For more than thirty-five years, her work has focused on the creation of gender-responsive and trauma-informed services. Her extensive experience includes designing women's services at the Betty Ford Center, developing programs for women and men in criminal justice settings, and being the featured therapist on the Oprah Winfrey Network TV show "Breaking Down the Bars." She also has served as a consultant to the United Nations Office on Drugs and Crime (UNODC) in Vienna and was selected for the federal Advisory Council on Women's Services.

Educated at Columbia University and the Union Institute, Dr. Covington has served on the faculties of the University of Southern California, San Diego State University, and the California School of Professional Psychology. She has published extensively, including ten gender-responsive, trauma-informed treatment curricula. One is *Voices: A Program of Self-Discovery and Empowerment for Girls*. Dr. Covington is based in La Jolla, California, where she is co-director of the Institute for Relational Development and the Center for Gender & Justice.

Roberto A. Rodriquez, MA, **LMFT, LADC** has more than fifteen years of experience in the field of addiction treatment. He holds a bachelor's degree in psychology and a master's degree in marriage and family therapy. He has worked in intensive outpatient settings and residential settings, with a focus on treatment for adolescents, men, couples, and families. He is the CEO of Family Recovery Resource Experts (FRrē) in Saint Paul, Minnesota, and is the founder of The Family Hub, a 501(3)c nonprofit created to deliver quality mental and behavioral services to underserved families in the Twin Cities.

Roberto is a coauthor of *Exploring Trauma: A Brief Intervention for Men,* with Dr. Stephanie Covington. Published by Hazelden, it is the only research-based intervention program related to trauma for men.

ADDITIONAL PUBLICATIONS

STEPHANIE S. COVINGTON

- *Awakening Your Sexuality: A Guide for Recovering Women*
- *Becoming Trauma Informed: A Training for Professionals* (variety of criminal justice and community editions available for use in US, UK, and Canada) (Facilitator's Guide, Participant's Workbook, and PowerPoint)
- *Beyond Anger and Violence: A Program for Women* (Facilitator's Guide, Participant's Workbook, and DVD)
- *Beyond Trauma: A Healing Journey for Women* (Facilitator's Guide, A Workbook for Women, and DVDs)
- *Beyond Violence: A Prevention Program for Criminal-Justice-Involved Women* (Facilitator's Guide, Participant's Workbook, and DVD)
- *Healing Trauma: A Brief Intervention for Women* (with Eileen Russo) (CD-ROM)
- *Helping Men Recover: A Program for Treating Addiction* (with Dan Griffin and Rick Dauer) (Facilitator's Guide and A Man's Workbook)
- *Helping Men Recover: A Program for Treating Addiction: Special Edition for Use in the Criminal Justice System* (with Dan Griffin and Rick Dauer) (Facilitator's Guide and A Man's Workbook)
- *Helping Women Recover: A Program for Treating Addiction* (Facilitator's Guide and A Woman's Journal)
- *Helping Women Recover: A Program for Treating Addiction: Special Edition for Use in the Criminal Justice System* (Facilitator's Guide and A Woman's Journal)
- *Leaving the Enchanted Forest: The Path from Relationship Addiction to Intimacy* (with Liana Beckett)
- *Moving from Trauma-Informed to Trauma-Responsive: A Training Program for Organizational Change* (with Sandra Bloom) (Facilitator's Guide and three DVDs)

- *Voices: A Program of Self-Discovery and Empowerment for Girls* (Facilitator's Guide and Interactive Journal)
- *A Woman's Way through the Twelve Steps* [Published in Spanish as *La Mujer y Su Práctica de los Doce Pasos*]
- *A Woman's Way through the Twelve Steps* (Facilitator's Guide and DVD)
- *A Woman's Way through the Twelve Steps Workbook* [Published in Spanish as *La Mujer y Su Práctica de los Doce Pasos Libro de Ejercicios*]
- *Women and Addiction: A Gender-Responsive Approach* (Manual and DVD)
- *Women in Recovery: Understanding Addiction* [Published in Spanish as *Mujeres en Recuperación: Entendiendo la adicción.*]

STEPHANIE S. COVINGTON AND ROBERTO A. RODRIGUEZ

- *Exploring Trauma: A Brief Intervention for Men* (CD-ROM)

For a list of Dr. Covington's recent articles and descriptions of her current seminars for professionals visit www.stephaniecovington.com and www.centerforgenderandjustice.org.